GET HIRED BY GOD

Inspiration At Work

Based on the teachings of
SIRSHREE

GET HIRED BY GOD

Based on the teachings of
Sirshree

Copyright © Tejgyan Global Foundation
All Rights Reserved 2012

Tejgyan Global Foundation is a charitable organization
with its headquarters in Pune, India.

ISBN : 978-81-8415-285-2

Published by WOW Publishings Pvt. Ltd., India
First Edition published in July 2012
Second Edition published in October 2022
Second Reprint February 2025

Printed and bound by Trinity Academy For Corporate Training Ltd, Pune

Copyright and publishing rights are vested exclusively with WOW Publishings Pvt. Ltd. This book is sold subject to the condition that it shall not by way of trade or otherwise, be lent, resold, hired out, or otherwise circulated without the publisher's prior written consent in any form of binding or cover other than that in which it is published and without a similar condition including this condition being imposed on the subsequent purchaser and without limiting the rights under copyright reserved above, no part of this publication may be reproduced, stored in or introduced into a retrieval system, or transmitted, in any form, or by any means, electronic, mechanical, photocopying, recording or otherwise, without the prior written permission of both the copyright owner and the above-mentioned publisher of this book. Any person who does any unauthorized act in relation to this publication may be liable to criminal prosecution and civil claims for damages.

Although the author and publisher have made every effort to ensure accuracy of content in this book, they hereby disclaim any liability to any party for any loss, damage, or disruption caused by errors or omissions, resulting from negligence, accident, or any other cause. Readers are advised to take full responsibility to exercise discretion in understanding and applying the content of this book.

*To all those great men and women
who served to convey the divine message of
Higher Consciousness to the masses,
thus serving God not just part time,
but full time.*

FOREWORD

"Men who do things without being told draw the most wages."

- Edwin H. Stuart

Man spends eight to ten hours on an average every day for work, which thus amounts to one third of his lifetime. He does it for sustaining himself and his family. His main focus is on survival and he looks at his job as a mere money making mechanism. However, once his physiological and safety needs are met, he takes pride in his job. He falls in love with it and his inspired body language in turn motivates others. He has harmonious relationship with people. At this stage some people question the purpose of such work and their life? From a mere personal outlook they transcend to an altruistic point of view. They work for the benefit of others.

Still there are few who question the ultimate purpose of success at work, the aim behind aim. Their sincere quest for truth makes them realize that success at work is only a stepping stone to the ultimate purpose of success. The ultimate purpose is to know who we truly are. When we realize our true nature as Consciousness, as the very Source of life, we use everyday life experiences to unleash our dormant potential and allow the Source to express its divine qualities through our body-mind. With this renewed understanding, the rigors and challenges at the workplace, which used to delude us earlier, can provide us with an opportunity to manifest higher qualities of the Source within us, like compassion, creativity, joy, patience and persistence, to name a few. Stabilized in our true nature, the Source, we work to awaken the blissful experience of the Source in everybody.

This book is based on the teachings of Sirshree on fulfillment and communication at the workplace. The guidance in the pages that follow will also help you to learn to enjoy, energize and elevate your work. When your feelings, thoughts, words and actions are aligned with whatever you do, then you are mastering the soul of work. Most people are unable to put their heart and soul into work due to negative feelings and thoughts about work and people at the workplace.

This book provides guidance on the principles of natural communication and effortless productivity. It helps bring about just the right changes in your attitude and thoughts. It teaches you how to have cordial relationships and harmony at the workplace by accessing the Source. Once you access the Source and learn to master your words and feelings at work, then they work for you in creating a fulfilling workplace. The insights given in this book will help you see work as a platform to unleash your hidden potential and allow the Source to work through you.

Sirshree's teachings on such a fulfilling life at the workplace, that he has imparted in a few of his discourses, has been woven into a fictional story that helps you learn the way to be in communion with the Source within you, so as to express its boundless potential.

Join Karmant, the central character of this story, as he progresses from being someone who is fed up with his job to becoming someone who learns to harness divine communication and intention at work, with a little help from Jeeodee.

PREFACE

"Don't just live for yourself. Don't just live for your job. Don't just live for others. Live for others because there is no other."

- Sirshree

Before you begin reading the fictional story in the pages that follow, understand various stages of labour and what sort of labour you are doing. Whether you are a chief executive officer (CEO) or a carpenter, you are doing one or the other form of labour. The work that a CEO does can be called the "Central Eye Opener." That is what the words CEO stand for.

Opening the eyes of the organisation and the people associated with the organisation is the labour that a CEO does. Each one of us is labouring — be it the mother at home or the manager at work. The question is what sort of labour you do. From the spiritual viewpoint, there are four stages of how one approaches work.

The first stage can be called "Survival Labour." Here one is merely working for the sake of himself/herself or for family. The only focus is on survival. Those who see their work as merely a money-making mechanism fall in this category. Their motto is "Live for yourself."

The next stage is "Inspirational Labour" where though the focus is on bread winning, there is pride in the job too. Let us understand this with an example. Once there were three labourers involved in breaking stones.

They were striking the stones with a massive hammer all day long under the hot sun for constructing their king's pet project. When they were asked what it is that they were exactly doing, the first labourer replied, "I am just carrying out what has to be done as per my miserable fate." "I am breaking stones for construction purposes," retorted the second labourer. When the third labourer was asked the same question, he said, "It is my privilege that I am building the temple, the pet project of our king." The third labourer had pride in his job. This is "Inspirational Labour," where you are inspired by your work and where your body language in turn inspires others. Those at this stage have fallen in love with their work. The motto of those at the second stage of labour is, "Live for your job."

Most people are stuck at the survival level or at the inspirational level. They do not look beyond. Let us see another example to understand this. Four friends had to use one boat to travel to a village. They sat in the boat and used the four oars to row all night. In the morning, they realized they had not moved at all. This is because they had not untied the boat. This is what happens at the first or second stage of labour. Though there is apparent effort, you have not really moved in life. It is important to move on.

The third stage of labour is "Impersonal Labour" — means labour that is not done only for personal benefit. It is not exclusive work — but inclusive, where you include the benefit of others. It is not individual labour, but universal in nature. The motto of those who are at this stage is, "Live for others."

Work done for the benefit of others is Impersonal Labour. But don't stop just there. Progress to the next stage. The fourth and final stage is "Liberational Labour." This is work that happens after you realize your true nature. After self realization, self expression follows. Here, work is not work at all. In this stage, labour arises from liberation. It is effortless effort. Stabilised in the Self (your true nature), you work for establishing the experience of the Self in everybody. You no longer live a selfish life. In fact, you live a "Self-ish" life — where the individual is transcended and one lives established in the Self. In the fourth stage, the motto is, "Live for others because, there is no other." The word Ashram (meaning hermitage) in Hindi exactly signifies this liberated labour that happens at this stage. "Shram" means labour. Ashram is absence of labour.

So, decide today to move towards the ashram. It does not mean you have to physically relocate to live in an ashram. It means you take an intention to move, at least, to the next level of labour from wherever you currently are. Have the intention to move from lamenting about your labour at the first stage to the next level of inspirational labour. If you are already at the second stage, take on an intention to move from yearning for labour to the next level of impersonal labour. If you are already at the third stage, take on an intention of moving from the desire of labouring for others to liberation.

1

"Working for this company is like being an insect trapped under a shoe. Either clients will pulverize you or your boss will squash you… either way, you're crushed," Karmant thought helplessly, slumping into his chair. Generally, Karmant was a man with a robust demeanor, with strong and broad shoulders. At work it was just the opposite. His usual posture at work was slouched in a chair with a grumpy look.

His eyes drifted over his overladen desk and the other expensive furniture fastidiously arranged on the 7th floor executive office of the most popular and hi-tech I.T. company in the state. Just then he heard a fragile voice from the door: "Good Morning, Sir. Please, may I come in?" Reena was Karmant's secretary. She was smart but timid. Petite and unassuming, she efficiently managed Karmant's paper work and his appointments.

"What's so good about the morning, Reena? Let's look at my calendar of appointments immediately. We have several client meetings lined up for the next few days," growled Karmant.

"Okay, Sir." Reena moved swiftly out of the office, taking the long list with her.

The day went by quickly, with Karmant sitting behind his desk mindlessly gnawing on burgers followed by potato chips and several cups of coffee.

Eyes glued to his computer screen, he spent the whole day worrying about Mr. Gupta and Mr. Malhotra.

The meeting with Mr. Malhotra was crucial and could not be missed. It was an immense opportunity for the company to get such a huge business deal. Karmant had to prove himself this time.

The evening passed by. He made frantic calls trying to get in touch with Mr. Gupta, but he was nowhere close to being reachable. Having consumed about eight strong cups of black coffee, Karmant was utterly drained and frustrated. He left for home.

On the way back he cursed the traffic and made up his mind that the world is a sad place to live.

He parked his car and shouted his lungs out at the watchman for having delayed in opening the front gate. Foul mood and irate vocabulary always escorted Karmant everywhere.

"Hi Karmant. Come in. How was your day? You look tired," greeted his wife, Bhavana.

He headed straight to his room to freshen up, growling at his five-year-old son. "How many times have I told you not to play with the papers kept near this telephone?" Karmant barked in reply. "Can't you understand when you're told once? You are so stupid and useless. Good for nothing!"

Raju, who had been engrossed in drawing pictures using colored sketch pens, was rattled. Tears welled in his eyes as he hurriedly gathered his sketch pens and ran crying to his mother for solace.

The dinner which normally followed was the same scene every day: either silence or angry words. Karmant never appreciated any delicious item on his platter. He would, as per routine, then have a drink, surf the TV channels, and go to bed in anticipation of the next day.

2

The next day arrived, accompanied by a tense atmosphere in the meeting room. The meeting with Mr. Malhotra had commenced.

"Mr. Malhotra, we have promised you great work and the best rates for this proposal. You have been our client for the past two years now. What changed your mind… I mean, what went wrong? Have we made a mistake somewhere? We can rectify any problems, and I can assure you…"

"No, Karmant. It's just that we have found a better deal with another vendor. His delivery schedule looks promising; your delivery schedules have always varied and have never been on time. I want to give this new vendor an opportunity. Of course, that doesn't mean that we are breaking any existing ties with your company. But I do want to make one other comment. We might have been more motivated to work out the delivery schedule issues, but your ill-tempered communication with my managers spoiled any chances of arriving at a mutually agreeable solution."

The deal had been called off. Karmant was immensely depressed. He closed the office door behind him and rested his head on the table.

A knock sounded at the door. "Come in," said Karmant, certain it was a message from the managing director.

It was Reena. "Sir, Mr. Desai wishes to see you in his office immediately," she said, with a concerned look at Karmant. She knew what was to come next. Karmant quickly collected himself and rushed to see Mr. Desai.

"May I come in, Mr. Desai?" Karmant inquired, standing with fear and worry at the office door.

"Yes, Karmant. Come in. So, I hear your meeting with Mr. Malhotra has failed."

"Yes. But what can be done? He was disappointed with the delivery schedule for the project. I can't help it if people here do not take their work seriously. It's their responsibility to give me work on time! I can't work on everything alone! And the absenteeism…"

"Well, Karmant…" Karmant went silent at his superior's steely tone. "Why don't you realize the reason we are losing business here? It's not because of the workers and their performance…" Mr. Desai's tone hit a crescendo, "…but because of YOU! It is YOU. YOU are the sole culprit for this failure. Have you ever heard yourself talk? Always frustrated, always tired. You never communicate the precise things at the right time and in the correct way. I believe you're unaware of what human relations are all about! All you do is blame others for your failures! Everyone complains about the way you talk to coworkers and the manner in which you lash out at your team. There's just one reason Mr. Malhotra did not consider this deal… because of the way you talk to his managers! I thought that you would realize this, but you haven't. Now I will have to take corrective steps. Please go back to work. See me tomorrow morning."

Karmant stood in shocked silence for a moment. "Fine." He stomped out of the office. Feelings of uselessness and failure gripped him.

Karmant took the same grumpy mood home with him. He spent the night sitting on his balcony facing the beach. He heard the roaring of strong waves hitting the shore. The darkness was not just in the sky; deep darkness had spread into his mind and into his life. He failed to see the shine of the moon and the stars in that darkness. With his mind fatigued from depressing thoughts, his eyes drooped, and he fell asleep.

The following morning, Karmant woke with a heavy heart and a heavy mind. Tension was etched into his face. He paid no attention to the innocent smile of his child, or to the caressing look of concern his wife had for him. Ignoring them, he mechanically got ready for work.

Engulfed in heavy feelings of tension and depression, his drive to the office was a sluggish one.

As he walked through the doors he felt the weight of glaring eyes. He noticed everyone at the office staring at him. He wondered what had happened. Finally, ignoring their glares, he stood at Reena's table. His face bore a worried and a questioning look.

"What's going on, Reena? What's the matter in the office? Has something serious happened?"

Reena dropped her gaze from Karmant's worried look to the ground below. Not understanding her expression, he walked towards his office. Everyone stood upright, watching him intently. As he lifted his hand to open the door of his office, he realized that the name plate on his office door was missing.

"You've been summoned by Mr. Desai, Sir. He wants to see you right away," the office aide ventured in a hushed voice. Trying to gather his thoughts, Karmant mustered his courage and answered, "Yes."

Knocking at Mr. Desai's door, he looked at the name plate. The importance of a name plate suddenly became apparent to him.

"Come in, Karmant." On stepping inside and standing to the front of the table, Mr. Desai signaled him to sit down. Karmant took his seat and looked at Mr. Desai with the same distressed look.

"Karmant, we had a board meeting yesterday… Uh… I know it may sound harsh but… let's put it plainly. The board has decided to give you an opportunity to work more closely with your team members. So…

you will be operating from the floor with them."

Looking into his face, astounded, Karmant shot back, "Have you demoted me?"

"Look, Karmant… if you look at this as something disrespectable, you won't learn anything from it; but look at it in a different way…"

"You are trying to tell me that just because you lost a silly, aggressive client, you have decided to demote me? I mean… this is so ridiculous! How can you behave like this? It's degrading and humiliating. I mean… just due to a deal? How insane can this be? Oh GOD, what in the world…"

"Well, in spite of hearing our repeated warnings to check your behavior, you have consistently ignored them. You've continued to inflict your moods and throw your tantrums around everyone on the floor and with the clients. I think, instead of being furious, you should be thankful that we have not fired you!"

"What! I can't believe this…"

"You can go home and think about the whole thing. Instead of getting wild and creating a scene, you may take today off. If you feel you can work as an associate of the research team, you can come back tomorrow and begin work. We will scrutinize your performance and your behavior for a period of three months. Following that, we shall make a final decision on your future with this organization. I still see a lot of potential in you, and so I request you not take this personally, but professionally."

Dumbfounded and angry, Karmant picked up his bags and barged out of the office, slamming the door behind him. Meeting the glares of his officemates he got all the more furious, and hastened out of the office into his car to go back home.

3

"How can I be demoted? Me? No way! They've lost their minds! They don't know what they're going to miss! I'm not going to work at the research level! I will quit the job instead of facing that humiliation." Such thoughts raced through Karmant's mind.

His early arrival at home surprised Bhavana.

"What happened to you? How are you home so early?" she asked anxiously.

"Why? Is there a problem? Can't I spend my time at home? Or do you feel uncomfortable with me around?"

"Why do you always talk so bitterly? Why can't you be kinder? You keep shouting all day long. Raju is also paranoid, afraid of being close to you! And…"

"Oh, don't start the same old rant again. I have better things to do than listen to you and Raju crying and complaining all the time!"

"I'm not complaining. Can't we just sit and talk?"

"No. I don't have time for all this. Please don't come into the study room. I have some important work to do." Saying this, he shut the study door with a bang.

Not understanding this behavior, Bhavana's eyes welled up with tears, but she forced them back for her son's sake. Seeing a frightened expression on little Raju's face, she pushed back her feelings and tried to help him get into a playful mood.

Karmant made frantic calls to all his friends, trying to find a place in one of their organizations. He was in a fit of desperation, clinging to the hope that his friends would empathize with his situation. Hours passed by, but despite words of assurance, there was no positive feedback from anyone. He realized that recession had set in everywhere, and he would have to stick with his organization. Shutting his eyes, he put his head down on the desk. Negativity, guilt, and depression crawled throughout him.

Night had fallen. Finding Bhavana and Raju already in bed, Karmant felt great relief. He stood out on the terrace to breathe some fresh air, and decided to go for a walk on the beach. The sound of the surf and the cool breeze reminded him of the many happy evenings he had spent with Bhavana on the beach. He was momentarily tempted to wake her up, but decided against it, since he would not have been able to look into her face. He walked down the beach with heavy feet, leaving behind his footsteps in the sand.

A huge rock sat in the middle of the beach. Karmant had seen people sitting on the rock and pondering their troubles in the past. Making sure that there were no sharp edges, he sat down to rest himself on the rock. The water washed at his feet, erasing the footsteps he had left behind.

"I wish life were that easy… that the waters of time would wash away the mistakes made in the sands of life," he thought. The peace of the beach and the serenity of the water had an unusual impact on him. Steeped in depression, he started to cry. "Why is success so difficult? What am I doing wrong? Is my way of thinking the problem? Why do I always mess up in communication? I don't mean harm to anyone. Why do such things happen in my life? Why do I always have to deal with people who make me feel irritated and angry? Does God really exist? If He does then why doesn't He bless me a peaceful life? Do I really always act worried and look tired? What should I change? Oh God… I am a real failure, a misfit in the office and at home as well. I haven't been a good father or a supportive husband. Being a good manager is farfetched. I'm just a real example of failure…"

He did not know when sleep hit him.

He woke up with a start when he heard a loud laugh.

"Ha hahahaha."

He opened his eyes and was stunned by what he saw. Towering above him was a ten-foot genie, right in front of his eyes. The fluorescent blue and white colors of the genie stood out vividly against the background of the dark sky.

Karmant was taken aback and fell off his feet, hitting the sand below with a hard thump. He shook with fear. "I don't believe this is real. Do genies exist? Are you real? How can it be possible? I didn't even rub a lamp or find a bottle."

Rubbing his eyes, he confirmed to himself that he wasn't dreaming. It was true! There was a genie clad in a suit and a tie, with a ponytail, standing right before him and staring down at him with an enigmatic smile.

The genie laughed aloud and replied, "A genie, or as they say jinn in Arabic, is nothing but a wild spirit. According to the Qur'an, God created jinn out of the 'fire of a scorching wind.' It wasn't until later that humans were made from mud and clay. We jinns are much more than demons or spirits. We're intelligent, free-willed creatures who live close to nature and are endowed with magical powers. We are very much like humans, only more supernatural. Some of us are good, some are evil, and still more are somewhere in-between. But the key is we can change our appearance at will…"

Dressed in formal attire, sporting a fluorescent red tie that stood out on his white shirt and black suit, the genie looked like a corporate mogul.

Karmant asked, "Is that why you are dressed in a suit?"

The genie replied, "Physical manifestations are but a choice. We jinns come in every shape and size, sometimes even without a head or a body. And your mind is playing a role here too… What is it that you seek? Do I appear like that?"

Karmant stared at the genie, still in disbelief and murmured to himself, "I seek liberation from my awful job… Is this why he is donning a formal official attire? But what can he do for me?"

"What can I do for you?" The genie smiled at Karmant.

Mustering some courage, Karmant replied, "I can ask you for anything that I want, and you will grant my wish?"

"Well, that actually depends on what you wish."

It was as if Karmant was waiting for someone to ask him this question. Hurriedly he replied, "I am very troubled with my life. I've been demoted, and I lost a big deal today, and everyone hates me for the way I talk to them… and… my family… Oh, there's so much of it to explain!"

"Well Karmant, relax. Take a breath."

Karmant took two deep breaths. Now, he was feeling relieved to some extent. He asked the genie, "How can I address you? Do you have a name? Or do you keep changing names as well?"

The genie laughed, "What's in a name? It's what we do that ultimately matters. You may call me Jeeodee."

"Jeeodee!!? That's a funny name. I have heard it for the first time. The name doesn't have a meaning."

"Do you know the meaning of your name, Karmant?"

"Now, what does the meaning of my name have to do with my problems?" Karmant thought to himself. With a puzzled look, he answered, "… But why?"

"The real meaning of Karmant is 'the end of *karma*.' That means the completion of each task undertaken. So, you just need to perform your task and everything else will be taken care of. But there is a deeper meaning to your name as well. Karmant means going beyond doing—*karma*—and non-doing—a-*karma*; just as *Vedanta* is transcending knowing—*veda*—and not knowing—a-*veda*, which is the knower of everything—the Source.

"I can't understand what you are saying. What is this Source?"

"The Source, you may call it as Consciousness, God or Self, is your true nature. It is the living, sentient principle dwelling within and around each and every one of us, because of which we are alive. This experience of beingness is constantly happening within every human being. It is the enlivening essence that exists beyond the mind, beyond the states of waking, dreaming and deep sleep. It is pure awareness, or pure wakefulness, due to which forms and phenomena come into existence. Your mind, comprising thoughts and feelings, is the expression of pure awareness. Our body is a denser, more obvious expression of the Source, a grosser expression of the subtler mind.

It is only due to the presence of Consciousness—the knowing principle—that your eyes can see; your ears can hear, your tongue can speak. And yes, it is due to its essential presence that thoughts arise!

The human body-mind is a vehicle through which the Source experiences life. More importantly, the human body-mind is an instrument that the Source employs to experience ***itself*** and express its divine qualities. So, Karmant, when you are connected with the Source within you and allow it to express through your body-mind, you see things happening effortlessly and spontaneously. Thus, you go beyond doing and non-doing as your name suggests."

"I'm able to get some idea of what you described as the Source, but I can't fathom what it means to go beyond doing and non-doing," Karmant said, with a frustrated look.

"Fine. Let's park that topic for now. Let's focus on your current problem. As you can see, I am a genie. I cannot help you fix your deals or make miracles for you. I believe that if one stabilizes on the Source, his true nature, and allows the Source to function through him, one can create miracles for oneself. I can, however, help you achieve all your goals and overcome your difficulties, with the help of right changes in your thoughts and attitude. If you want, I can teach you ways to access the Source so as to be in communion with it and allow it to express through you. This will lead you to discover the principles of natural communication and effortless productivity. If you practice them in your everyday life, I am sure you will be able to overcome all your difficulties. Above all, people will begin to love you for the way you deal with them. You will become an inspiration for others."

"But how is this possible…? I am not able to sustain myself, how can I be inspiration for others? This is easier said than done. I have so many problems. Can he really solve all of them…? I can't believe this. But I don't have any options left now. None of my friends are helping me to get a job. Help is farfetched; they are not even accepting my calls. Here, at least he is offering me help. Let's see what he says," Karmant thought to himself.

He said, "Really! Is that really possible? Could you please teach me everything I need to know to make things right? I want to be more successful in my life and at work. I want to be loved by my family."

"Certainly! What is your problem?"

"I just got demoted, because I lost a business deal. Everyone says that I don't behave well. Now, I can't face the humiliation of being demoted. How can I work with the people I once instructed? I can't do this!"

The genie adjusted his tie. "All that you have to do is work on two simple aspects. What I shall tell you tonight will reveal the secret of remaining calm and in control when you speak. We can call it the 'Stepping Stone'."

4

Karmant was still dazzled by the sight of the genie, but was eager to learn anything that could help him out of his troubles. He sat down on the soft sand and waited intently for him to begin.

"I will now explain to you the four ways of solving your problem. You can select any one of them. Are you ready?"

"I'm all ears." Karmant answered enthusiastically.

"Okay, listen carefully. Many people in situations like yours wonder if they should continue with their present job or if they should quit. There are four ways to solve this dilemma. You can select any one of the options that suits you. Here's the first option: whenever you face something which doesn't interest you, you quit it."

"Oh no! How can I quit? This job is my livelihood. It's my means for supporting my family. I can't quit."

"Exactly! Your answer shows consideration. Some people often want to quit their jobs and hop onto new jobs for small reasons. They never stick to one place. I am mentioning this to you as an option to weigh, so you can decide for yourself."

"Okay… yeah," Karmant said in contemplation.

"The second option is to change something in your current job. Speak to your boss and get yourself assigned to a different division. Take on goals you have not taken on before. Do something in your current organization that excites you."

"Well, this option won't work for me now. In my present situation, I can't bargain for a change in my job duties."

"Then, the third option is to accept your job. Once we accept things, they no longer hold the power to trouble us. Also, the third option is kind of a precursor to the fourth option."

"Oh…?" Karmant was listening intently.

"The fourth option is to change your perspective towards the work you do. The outlook you take towards your work is extremely important. When you look at your work from a higher perspective, you will realize that it is helping you to develop intellectually, to learn things required for your future, and to become prepared physically as well as mentally. If you understand the technique of taking the higher perspective, you will be able to work anywhere in the world."

"I did not fully understand the fourth option," Karmant said with a puzzled look on his face.

"How can you change your perspective in your way of working to rekindle your interest? Think over it. There is no work in the entire universe which cannot be made interesting. Some people dislike math, but when they start working on it, playing with it, experimenting with it, they slowly discover their liking for it.

Think of a truck driver who finds his job very monotonous. To make his job more interesting, he can imagine his job as a video game, in which the player gains points by following traffic rules and avoiding accidents. If he takes a correct turn, or moves to the side in time, or stops at a zebra crossing, or drives without unnecessary honking, he can give himself points. By changing his mind-set, he will be able to enjoy his job as well as perform well. Earlier he might have become enraged when other drivers cut him off or failed to signal, but now even as he shouts at them he can think of it as part of the game. What was once felt to be a burdensome job will now be interesting."

"This is fun. I never imagined that something so creative could be applied even to a driver's job!" exclaimed Karmant.

"But remember, you can't get to the fourth till you go through the third option. Unless you accept your current job, you will not be able to change your perspective. Acceptance precedes change in perspective."

"Well, the third solution suits me best. I will select that and would like to explore it. I have a hard time accepting things and that is what causes the biggest hurdles in my job."

"Okay… Let me elaborate on this answer for you. In life, we come across many unwanted situations and people that make us unhappy. There is a small but very powerful mantra that can change your life dramatically and bestow peace and happiness on you. The mantra is: ***Can I accept this?***

'This' can be anything which is affecting you, either from outside or from within you. If any unwanted incident has occurred or if you have to deal with an unpleasant person, just ask yourself, 'Can I accept this?'

In this way, when you accept a situation or a person, your power to deal with them will increase enormously. You will find that the answer will be a 'Yes' in almost 100% of small incidents. It is only because you fail to ask yourself this question that you automatically retreat to your shell. With this mantra, you will never live a constricted life; instead, you will open up to everything that is bothering you. The moment you say 'yes', you will notice that negative emotions and all thoughts drop and you dip into the Source automatically, though just for a few moments. This little mantra can work wonders."

Karmant wanted to have the solution to his demotion, and here the genie was asking him to accept the demotion itself. His temper surged.

He yelled at the genie, "Are you trying to tell me that I should ask myself if I can accept the demotion?"

"Karmant, what did really happen? Were you actually demoted? Was your salary brought down?"

"I have been asked to work with those who once reported to me."

"Okay then, accept that particular directive. You must make use of this mantra. When you are able to accept that you have been asked to work with those who once reported to you, you will be able to look beyond its problems and pain. You will be freed to consider how you could possibly learn from them and get back to how things were. Accept it as a process that you have to go through willingly to emerge successful from it. You need to use it as a stepping stone."

Karmant bit back his anger and replied, hesitantly, "But what if my answer to the question is NO. No, I can't accept it?"

"With this mantra, if the answer is 'No, I can't accept this,' then you must accept the non-acceptance as well. Let me help you understand by using an example. Suppose you dislike a person and whenever you see him, you say to yourself, 'I just can't tolerate this man's face.' Ask yourself, 'Can I accept my non-acceptance?' If your answer is yes, you can control your reactions to him. Or, if you are worried and that worry is constantly eating into you, just ask yourself, 'Can I accept this worry?' When your answer is, 'Yes, I am worried. I can accept it,' you no longer compound your troubles by worrying about the worry.

When you accept your non-acceptance, something new comes to fore. When you start accepting yourself and your faults, you will be at ease with yourself. It will also be easier for you to accept others and their faults as well."

Karmant still had one or two things troubling him about this approach. He replied, "I think I understand. But if I accept everything, how can things change if they are truly wrong?"

The genie smiled patiently. "You must definitely change the situation if it is wrong, but you can't do so without unlocking both your hands. Your first step to solve the problem must be to accept that problem. Upon doing so, you are able to look beyond the grief and the worry that problem has brought into your life, and you open up to ways of resolving it. Acceptance is not about being submissive or passive to what is happening in the world. With acceptance, all things get absorbed easily; they don't harden into an enclosure that stays within you. On the other hand, by resisting you energize 'that' what you don't want in your life. What you resist, persists. Resistance is the source of all sorrow, while acceptance is liberation from all sorrow.

Life is like a river. Rivers have banks; that is how a river is contained. If you dissolve those boundaries the water will evaporate. Likewise, sorrow collects between boundaries formed in your life. This unhappiness will vanish when you restrict the formation of any boundaries.

Boundaries are a symbolic representation of the limitations of our mind. Dissolve them, and there will be no accumulation of any sorrow."

Now, this sounded logical to Karmant. He exclaimed, "I had never thought of it this way before. I would always get annoyed when my expectations were not met and I was never able to accept things the way they are. I have a new way and a new mantra to help me now. But… sometimes, whether I accept something or not, I can't stop my mind from constantly running over the pros and cons of it. I get tired and angry when I'm burdened with thoughts like that. What should I do?"

"Do you realize that when your thoughts are troubled, your communication with others also becomes troubled?"

"Yeah, I think so. When I am troubled, I shout and get angry with people, and use harsh words with them."

"Focus more on what you are doing, instead of becoming preoccupied with talking. Your work will speak for itself and will bring about the good communication you desire."

"But how can I achieve that type of focus?"

"First, tell me what thoughts are?"

"What kind of a question is that? Thoughts are thoughts!"

"Let me make it easy for you. We can define thoughts as the communication that we do with ourselves. Or maybe, a better terminology: say, self-talk."

Karmant paused for a moment, running this over in his mind. He began to smile. "Yes, I see what you're saying. Thoughts are nothing but the communication that takes place within ourselves! Wow! Now I'm understanding the depth of what you're saying. I've never heard anyone put it like that. You are really a genius, Genie!"

The genie laughed a deep, jolly laugh. "Thank you! Okay, now tell me this: do you control yourself, or do you let yourself be controlled by others? If you allow yourself to be controlled by others, it means you've placed the remote control of your life into the hands of someone else. When you operate from the Source, you live a disciplined and content life and your remote control remains in your own hands.

A person communicates with other people through language, but with himself through self-talk. Self-talk is nothing but quiet communication with ourselves by way of the thoughts that run in our heads. So, self-talk is the communication we use within ourselves. It is important to work on saying the right things to oneself and others."

Karmant was taken aback. "But while talking to myself, I say only the right things… correct?"

"If a person happens to make an error in his choice of words while talking to another person, the people around him—such as parents, friends, teachers, and well-wishers—immediately correct him. However, when the same person says wrong words to himself, there is no one to correct him. As we grow up, we learn the art of right conversation with the external world. However, most people never learn the art of effective self-talk due to two reasons:

1. They probably never even realize the need to learn it.
2. They usually never come across anybody who has mastered this skill and can act as a guide for them."

Karmant became excited again. "Yes, I see what you're saying. All day long, I'm so busy with my office work that I rarely get time to think about thinking. I never ask myself if I'm saying the right things to myself!"

"Yes! It is vital that self-talk is done in the right way. It is only through improving the technique of self-talk that we can improve our relationships and achieve all-round self-development. That's the magic we possess inside us.

We need to learn the vocabulary of self-talk. There are words that must be repeated and words that must be avoided in self-talk. In our conversations with others, we avoid abusive words to maintain harmonious relationships. Likewise, you need to cast away negative thoughts in order to sustain harmony and a healthy relationship with yourself.

You must understand the importance of punctuation in self-talk. You must know where to insert a comma, or where a full stop is required. Good self-talk technique lets you communicate correctly with yourself, and maintain mental peace. This positivity then gets reflected in your behavior towards others. This combination of good self-talk and good use of speech can be called perfect communication. When you achieve perfect communication, that will become your reputation. 'Can I accept this?' is a good example of correct punctuation in your self-talk."

5

With Karmant now paying rapt attention, the genie continued to speak words of encouragement and motivation to him.

"Everyone wants to know how their miseries can be brought to an end and how difficulties in life can be overcome. Good self-talk is the secret behind it. To have a good self-talk, follow these principles:

1. No incident is joyous or sorrowful in itself. Feelings of joy or sorrow stem from the self-talk that begins at the time of the incident.
2. You create your world with your self-talk. The root of all sorrows is nothing but self-talk. Your self-talk creates heaven or hell for you.
3. Nobody can make you unhappy unless you let them.
4. Just as man's difficulties lie within him, so do the solutions.
5. Negative self-talk generates negativity in you. In turn, that negativity flows into your communication with others, through your expressed feelings and words."

"But when I come across failure, or difficult people at work, or situations that I can't handle, what kind of self-talk should I do then?" asked Karmant, thirsting for answers.

"That's an important question, and we have already looked at the answer. Whenever any event occurs in your life that you feel you can't handle, ask yourself, 'Can I accept this?' The answer will usually be 'Yes'. It will help you dip into the experience of the Source. When you operate from the Source, events in your life will automatically steer their course towards the ultimate goal of life. As a result, your self-talk will change. It will save you in all ups and downs of your life, at all times. You will change your perspective or take the required action happily without being a victim."

"I see. I can see how punctuating negative self-talk with the question 'Can I accept this?' is an excellent formula. Do you also have success formula that I can use? Please tell me if you have one," urged Karmant.

"The best formula for success is to get rid of all notions of success you carry."

"Notions of success!?" Karmant was baffled.

"Yes. People on Earth have many presumptions about success. They say, there can be no success if you are not well-educated; people can't be successful if they are not fluent in English; only lucky people become successful; good references and contacts are necessary to become successful; without a spouse to support you, you can't achieve success; only those born into a wealthy family can be successful... there is no end to myths like these. In reality, there are many examples of successful people who did not have an abundance of capital or knowledge, and yet made it to the top by relying on their ability to inspire others. Any of these factors can prove to be helpful for attaining success, but none are the prerequisite for success."

"If you say all of these are presumptions, then what is the reality?"

"Be happy. Change your self-talk. Punctuate your negative self-talk. When you are happy, you are automatically propelled towards your highest potential."

Karmant thought this over for a moment and then leaned forward. "Let me run some of my own beliefs by you. Can you tell me if they are correct or incorrect? I've always taken for granted that it takes a lot of time to be successful. I also believe that success comes only with experience, and experience implies a lot of hard work. Also, if I am not able to complete my work on time, I feel like I'm unsuccessful and can never be a success." His expression darkened as he remembered the feelings of failure that had dogged him throughout his career, even as others praised him for his success.

The genie's voice was gentle. "Even these are misconceptions about success. People have become successful irrespective of their age, background and upbringing. If others can do it, so can you.

The purpose of making you aware of these myths is so that you can get rid of them. If you are stuck in any of these myths, success will surely elude you. If you remain free of such wrong beliefs, you will find success at your doorstep very soon.

Opportunity knocks at your door in various disguises. Every problem and every difficulty is an opportunity disguised in the garb of unhappiness and discomfort. Often opportunity knocks on the back door, when you don't expect it. Be aware of every opportunity that knocks at your back door.

Now, coming to your feelings of failure over incomplete work: don't punish yourself in this situation. By doing so you only build more boundaries within your mind, and make future successes even more difficult. You don't have to depend upon completion of all activities to be successful. That's trying to derive success through external means. You can be successful even if your activities are incomplete, because your internal state is more important. When you feel complete and content from within, irrespective of the status of your activities, you will progress towards your highest potential."

"You've blown my mind with this advice, Genie. All my life, I have struggled hard to complete every last activity on time in an attempt to be successful. In the process, I have worn away my strength and my happiness. I've been harsh to people when they didn't seem to work as hard as me. I've even been harsh with them when they appeared to be more content than me. I realize now that I have never been content with myself."

Karmant sighed deeply, processing this new revelation. Then he turned his attention back to the genie. Something in his demeanor had become brighter. He no longer looked like the downtrodden, defeated man who had trudged to the shore hours earlier.

"Thank you so much. I am so happy that I learned all this today. I will never let these beliefs become a barrier for me again. Can I get my diary to note down all the advice you've given me? Will you wait here until then?"

"No. Our talk for today is complete. I must go now. But remember—happiness is a prelude to achieving your highest potential. Acceptance is the first step towards it, and right self-talk is the next."

"Oh no! I need to hear more from you!"

"Instead, why don't you immediately start practicing what you have heard already?"

"But how?"

"Simply by accepting that our talk is over for today." The genie winked at Karmant.

Despite himself, Karmant laughed. "You really are smart. Okay… I think I can accept this. But what about the other lessons that you promised to teach me?"

"We can meet here again to discuss them tomorrow. Meanwhile, you can practice all that you've learned at your office."

"Will it really work?"

"Try it and tell me. For now, goodnight! Have a nice day at the office."

"Okay… Thanks. I will meet you here again tomorrow. But… Hey, wait! How can I reach you? Should I call out to you?"

"You can reach me on this rock. Get to this rock and practice this simple meditation and I will promptly arrive.

Close your eyes and relax. Take a deep breath in, and exhale out. Now, concentrate on what's going on in your mind. Watch your thoughts. Do not dwell on your thoughts, or become entangled in them. Simply watch them come and go, like a puff of cloud passing through clear skies.

Now, as you watch your thoughts, start numbering them. Number each thought as it arises, and then let it go, without holding on to it or further thinking about it. Do not evaluate or answer any thought, but simply number each and let it pass by. Even if you think that you have no thought, number that as a thought as well. Go on like this until you count up to twenty, and I will have arrived." The genie winked at him and flashed a dazzling smile.

"Okay. I will practice this. Sounds odd… however, I will give it a try tomorrow. You promise to be here when I do this, right?"

"Yes, Karmant. I promise. Be assured."

Whoooshhhh….

The genie disappeared into the night.

Karmant tip-toed into the house and retired to his bed with a light and positive mind. For the first time in a long time, his eyes twinkled with the first glimpse of the bright stars in the dark night. His eyes closed, after some time, with the shine closely guarded in them.

6

Karmant began the new day with a smile in his thoughts and a twinkle in his eyes. He decided not to disclose his night-time talk with the genie to Bhavana. Reserved, but peaceful, he prepared himself for the day and left for work.

His mind started to swirl with worries about how the day would go and filled with anxious chatter. "I wonder what people will think of me now… They'll think I'm a loser… Oh no!" But he remembered genie's words and reminded himself to practice good self-talk. "I accept being demoted and I will work hard from now on to regain what I have lost."

Reassured and strengthened by this positive self-talk, he opened the door to Mr. Desai's office. Yesterday he had closed the same door with anguish.

"Good Morning! I accept my demotion and I wish to return to work without embarrassing myself any further. I am ready to get started."

Mr. Desai was stunned by Karmant's change of attitude. He couldn't understand this new radical acceptance. "Okay. I will let the manager know to make room to accommodate you in his team. In the meantime, you can make arrangements to shift there."

"Certainly," said Karmant. He drifted away from the door into the open floor area, where he met the same defiant looks that had targeted him the day before.

"What!? Do I look like an alien to you all?" he said loudly, with irritation in his voice.

Everyone commenced work with sarcastic smiles on their lips.

He settled behind his new desk with feelings of embarrassment. His new boss approached and gestured him into an empty office for a quick talk.

"Hi Karmant! I am Jay. I lead this team. You'll be reporting to me. So… make yourself comfortable, and if you need any help, ask."

Karmant's temper flared. "I know you lead the team, but I think you've forgotten that I was the project manager! I don't need any help from you, or any of the team members. So just buzz off and let me do my work!" Karmant stalked away.

"The same old arrogant Karmant! No change! What a pity," thought Jay.

Now Karmant's mind was crowded with angry thoughts. "What the hell do they think of themselves? Treating me like I'm dumb… don't they know what position I held! This whole thing is so embarrassing…"

He caught himself and took several deep breaths. "Oh no, I'm doing it again. Okay, get calm… cool down… self-talk, self-talk. Improve, improve, Karmant. Accept the things that have come… Phew!"

Trying to control the nomadic tendencies of his mind, he sat down in his new chair. The chair's back was much lower and didn't support his back like his earlier chair. Looking at the new constrained place around him filled him with annoyance.

"So, how's the new place, KARMANT?" an associate to his left commented sarcastically, intentionally using Karmant's first name in order to show disrespect.

A growl rose in Karmant's throat, and his face flushed. "Don't you know who I am? It's SIR, not KARMANT, you arrogant jackass! I'll mess with your appraisals …"

"Hold on, hold on. Did you just mention appraisals? I think you've forgotten where you are sitting now, KARMANT! This is just the way you humiliated us. It's your turn now. So get ready for fun, all day, everyday." He smiled wickedly. The others in the office stretched their necks to look at Karmant and started smiling along with the associate.

Picking up his files, Karmant approached Jay and demanded to be shifted, but it was to no avail. It was the strict order of the managing director to make him sit at that desk among his former subordinates.

With feelings of hatred and anger welling up in his nerves, he headed for a scheduled team meeting. Suddenly, he once again remembered the mantra: "Can I accept this?" The thought brought him some composure. Whatever had already happened that day and whatever was to come, he resolved to remain positive in his thoughts and words.

7

"Gentlemen, we are here to discuss the details of the project and its deadline. We have an important meeting on the 15th of next month, where the client will review our work, so we have to ensure that we are prepared for it. So, this meeting was called to finish the designated work before the end of the month, and submit it to the Quality Assurance team for review, so it can be taken up at the client meeting. Karmant, Suresh will hand your work over to you. Suresh, make sure you do that before lunch today. Okay. Does anybody have any questions?"

"No…" said the whole group, and everyone moved to their desks to get started.

During lunch time Karmant sat at his desk and worked continuously. As usual, people stared at him, no matter what he did. He did not talk to anyone in the team, and decided that from then on he'd stay aloof during lunch.

As the whole day passed by in silence, he felt a slight depression setting into him. But he set his mind to accept the new location and the new work, and by the end of the day he was quite comfortable with his environment.

That evening Karmant had a quiet dinner by himself. As the sky changed its color to darker shades, he waited until Bhavana and Raju fell asleep.

With silent footsteps, he headed to the far end of the beach. He perched upon the same old rock as before and closed his eyes. He tried to recollect the thought-numbering meditation the genie had taught him, but frustration arose in him. "This is difficult… watching thoughts." He suddenly realized that even that was a thought! He slowly began numbering them. While he almost became lost many times in the details of his thoughts, the anticipation of his appointment with the genie kept surfacing and constantly reminded him to stay focused. When he was just about to number his fifteenth thought, a subtle shiver ran through the rock. The shaking increased until his teeth began to chatter. All at once, the shaking ceased and the genie appeared out of nowhere, towering over him.

"Hello Karmant!"

"Ah! I thought you wouldn't come. It was taking so much effort to number my thoughts. I thought it would take me all night long to reach twenty."

"Don't worry; this is just the beginning. With practice you will become efficient at concentrating, and will become adept at detaching from your thoughts. This skill will greatly assist you in the future. So, how was your day?"

"It was okay. It left me feeling a little depressed."

"That's fine. You have accepted that you are feeling depressed, haven't you? Now, go ahead and find the solutions to your problem and come out of that depression."

"But how? I can't see any solution."

"Alright then… I'll help you uncover it! Tell me what happened at work today. Didn't the two lessons work?"

Karmant looked at the shoreline sheepishly. "They did work. In fact, I was very receptive today, and I did accept my demotion. But now my coworkers are bothering me. They are being rude to me. They say I used to treat them that way, but they're being unbelievably rude. It makes me really angry."

"That's okay. It doesn't sound like much of a problem."

Karmant's temper flared. "How can you say that? Easy for you to say, you don't have to face it!"

The genie held up his hands in a conciliatory gesture. "Okay…okay… Relax first, and then we'll talk calmly about it. Look: since you behaved badly with them, they will want to get even with you now. They would want you to experience the pain they've felt. What you give comes back to you manifold. If you give love, you will get love. Once you show them that you are changing, slowly they will accept you. When you show them kindness, they will want to be friends with you. They will start loving you. But you must be the one to extend the first step towards them."

"But how should I do that? They make me so irritated. I just can't control my anger; I have to retaliate. But they bounce it right back at me. Earlier, since I was a project manager, they couldn't say much; but now that I've been demoted things are worse. I can't control my anger at home either. Bhavana always feels bad when I am angry, but I can't help myself. I get so furious, I just lose my sense and blurt out whatever occurs to me. I realize my mistake later, but by then she is already upset. When I arrive at home and see all the toys scattered everywhere, I just can't tolerate it. I yell at Raju. Even though I want to spend quality time with my wife and son, invariably I spoil the mood. It's become so bad that I have decided to remain silent and simply not talk to anyone."

"I see. Let's learn some new techniques today to help you overcome your anger and break your silence."

"Do you really think there's a way for me to control my bad temper? I don't believe in counting 1 to 100 and drinking cold water. It never works. You can't possibly have cold water by your side every time you get into an argument, and neither can I imagine counting to 100 when I'm speaking with someone in the office."

"We will look at this in a different way. We will understand what exactly anger is, and how to take charge of it."

"What does this have to do with teaching me how to be a successful and effective communicator?"

"It's very simple. Just as self-talk and acceptance help you gain control over your thoughts and talk positively with yourself, so does controlling anger. If you are able to keep your anger in check, you are holding the key to successful, calm, and peaceful communication with your colleagues.

If you stop getting angry at people, you won't waste time and energy with fights. You will be able to communicate the right things in the right way to them. You will be able to think rationally. Above all, you will win the support of all your teammates.

When you get angry you use harsh words, and miscommunication happens. This spirals into a series of reactive behaviors and words."

"So, how can I control my anger?"

"Let's first understand what anger is, and the way it is expressed. Anything obstructing the fulfillment of one's desires causes anger. Some people seethe with anger; they burn inside with the fire of anger, though they may not get violent or scream or shout. There are others who blurt out their anger. When they get angry, they use profanity; they insult others, shout, scream, or even go as far as being violent and abusive. If they are not able to control others with their words, then they start throwing and breaking things. Their only intention is to get the other person in agreement with them, by any means. If they can't control the other person, at least they want to impress their displeasure upon them."

"Yes. I understand this. Perhaps I get angry for… some of the same reasons as well."

"Anger also means punishing yourself for others' mistakes. Whenever one sees another's mistake, he gets angry. But he forgets this truth: by getting angry he is punishing and torturing himself."

"How can that be? When I get angry, I don't feel that I am punishing myself. At the time, I feel that getting angry is justified to show my displeasure," Karmant said confidently.

"Think of this example. When we put sugarcane into a crusher, the crusher gets to taste the sweetness first, and only later do others get to enjoy the sweet juice. But if we put stones in the crusher, then it will be the crusher that gets damaged first. Your body is like the crusher, and the stones are thoughts of anger. Anger harms you first. If you curse somebody, then it may or may not negatively affect the other person, but it will certainly affect you."

"But when I get angry, I get a burst of energy to solve my problems. My body has not been damaged in any way."

"Okay. Let me explain it to you with some scientific data. When you get angry, your heart rate, arterial tension, and testosterone production increase, the stress hormone called cortisone decreases, and the left hemisphere of your brain becomes more stimulated. In the long run you may have health problems, like headaches, problems with digestion, insomnia, anxiety, depression, high blood pressure, skin problems… even heart attacks and strokes. Not only that, but anger can lead to other negative emotions, like bitterness, hopelessness, futility, and overall sadness. Let's face it: it's hard to have a good time if you're holding on to anger."

Karmant laughed despite himself. "My friend, you are very good at making big lists of everything! Yes… Now, I get your point. Anger is a self-imposed punishment. When we slap someone, the first thing that gets hurt is our hand. If we lash out at someone, we first harm ourselves. Right?"

The genie laughed heartily. "You've got the point. When you understand that when you use harsh words or get angry, you are actually punishing yourself first, you can easily get rid of this habit.

You must also understand about the ego. Ego and anger are two beasts: one is white, and the other is black. The white beast does not look as bad as the black one, because the color white is subtle but black stands out prominently. When somebody's ego is hurt, he gets angry. Anger is the effect, but ego is the cause. Anger is the symptom and ego is the disease."

"Okay… I understand what you are saying. I get angry because my ego gets hurt. When I get angry, I feel a surge of energy within me. I feel like I should just silence the other person. I try to get an upper hand on whatever he says. That desire comes from my ego, correct?"

"Yes, Karmant. You are doing well."

"Tell me something, then. I speak harsh words in a fit of rage. I lose control over my words at such times. I just blurt out whatever comes to me. But it's only words, right?"

"On the contrary, if you take a look at history, angry words have led to wars! The epic war of Mahabharata was a result of Draupadi's humiliating words to Duryodhana, when she said, 'Blind fool! Like father, like son.' Words spoken without awareness can lead to destruction. Even today, you can witness terrorism seething amongst some nations, which leads to war. All of this is due to differences of opinion. Many prisoners repent for the crime they committed, because they realize much later that a moment of anger has destroyed their lives. Anger is momentary madness."

"That does sound familiar. Look; I have repented too many times after my bouts of anger, but I always go back to the same old behavior. But today the impact is clearer than before. I do want to eliminate anger from my words and my behavior."

"Anger is not always destructive. You can use anger constructively. Say a person is distressed by the heat. He then sets out to create something which will put an end to his distress, and he invents a fan. That was a constructive use of anger!"

"This is quite interesting! So, how can I get rid of my destructive anger?"

"There are several techniques through which you can pause before speaking or expressing your anger. Take a deep breath; practice forgiveness; give people a chance to explain their mistakes or their opinion before you speak; try to step into others' shoes to see their reasoning. When you explain things or ask for an explanation, assumptions and miscommunications can dissolve easily. Wait for others to finish before you give them your opinion."

"Phew... I thought you would just go on with your list. It sounds like taking deep breaths would be the easiest option to start with. Could you please explain more about that?"

"Sure! When you are angry, start taking deep breaths. If you can make it to this point, then you can win over your anger. You will then become aware of the present moment. In fact, the emotion of anger emerges not for you to be angry, but rather for you to read it. When you are angry, consult with the sensations of your body to see what is exactly happening to it. You may find that your eyes are getting red, fists are clenching, breathing is becoming shallow and rapid, or your heart is beating faster. Try to focus on these symptoms and you will see that your anger vanishes."

"Okay, I can do that. Now, you also talked about forgiveness. Many times I've realized my mistake only after the other person has gone away. By that point, even if I want to apologize, I stop myself. In fact, I very rarely say sorry in person. So, I don't think the forgiveness technique works for me."

"Hold on, Karmant. Let me explain what true forgiveness is all about. You can practice forgiveness even if you are unable to say sorry in person. You can mentally picture that person later and imagine apologizing to him for all the trouble you've caused, can't you?"

"Yes, I can do that. That's not a big deal!"

"Good. So, now that you are ready to seek forgiveness at the mental level, practice forgiveness prayer every night before going to bed. Recall all the people whom you have hurt, and seek forgiveness from them from the bottom of your heart. You can pray words like these:

'I seek forgiveness from you.

Please forgive me for the hurt I caused you

through my words, actions, feelings, or thoughts.

I will ensure that I don't commit such mistakes again.'

Recall all the people you carry grudges against, and let go of the grudges by saying:

'I am letting go of the hatred, resentment, or complaints

that I have held in my mind against you.

I forgive you. I love you. I respect you.

I seek forgiveness for carrying a grudge against you.

Please forgive me.'

When you practice forgiveness you will be freed from the negative feelings caused by anger, hatred, resentment, envy, depression, and fear. Your relationships with others will improve.

Even so, don't presume that you are doing anyone any favors by forgiving them; you are only helping yourself."

Karmant looked surprised at this last sentence, but as he turned the idea over in his mind he nodded. "I never thought about it that way. But, what if I do have the opportunity to confront the other person?"

"It's important to control your anger before you express your opinions, so you can give a calm explanation. Imagine stepping into the other person's shoes; understand his viewpoint. Be polite, frank, and honest when you express your thoughts. If you've made a mistake, accept your culpability. If it's the other way round, and another person has offended you and expresses remorse, learn to forgive and give him a chance. But in any situation, never use harsh words. Don't tell somebody that he is looking sick and tired, or that he's hopeless. Your words may become the cause of anger or root of some disease; not just in that other person, but in yourself as well.

You should prepare your body to support you when you face stressful situations where you need to control your anger. Learn to calm down and relax. Spend some time with yourself and with family. Do things that you like to do. Eat fruits and good food. Exercise regularly. Practice meditation. For now, practice the thought-numbering meditation I taught you. Meditation makes the restless mind quiet. Express your feelings to your reliable close ones. You may also write your feelings in a diary. Letting out your feelings in a safe way allows you to be free of them."

Karmant felt slightly overwhelmed at this advice, but at the same time, he felt energized. "These are wonderful techniques. I'll start using them right away at my office tomorrow. I want to show people that I am a good person, and a good leader that can take care of them."

The genie nodded encouragingly. "Always remember: there is no need to shy away from people or stop communicating with them. Non-communication is one of the worst forms of communication. Always communicate, whether with your clients, at home, or with your coworkers. When you keep silent, the other person begins to assume things about you, and this leads to miscommunication."

"Okay, I understand. Let me try this tomorrow at the office."

"Alright! I will see you again tomorrow, Karmant… and I will expect to hear good news!"

"Yes, my friend. Thank you for all you've done to help me! I will look forward to seeing you tomorrow."

Karmant swayed joyfully as he returned to his room. He practiced the forgiveness prayer before going to bed. He felt carefree now, relieved of the anxiety and stress that usually plagued him at night, and eager to put all he had learned into practice.

As he watched the twinkling stars from his window, he felt his happiness was reflected in them. He thanked the genie from the bottom of his heart. Feeling gratitude for the softness of the pillow, he fell asleep peacefully. Soon he was lost in sweet dreams.

8

With a twinkle in his eyes, a smile on his lips, and a look of calmness on his face, Karmant was getting ready for work. Bhavana couldn't help but stare when she saw him. "Wow, Karmant… You are looking handsome today." Admiring himself in the mirror, Karmant was amazed to see his own reflection. He wished he could be identical to this reflection forever. If it had not been for the genie, he wouldn't have been able to sail through the turbulent waters of his stormy life. Within his thoughts he thanked the genie wholeheartedly.

All these years, he had forgotten what it was to be at leisure. Peacefully, he finished all his morning chores. He had breakfast with Bhavana. He couldn't remember the last time he had breakfast with her. Bidding farewell to her, he left home for another unprecedented office day. The hustle at the office today no longer annoyed him. Throughout the morning he was able to keep his anger under wraps using the techniques the genie had taught him, and he managed to get along with everyone.

His colleagues were surprised by his calm composure. Some were eager to know the secret behind it. Others resented him for it.

"Hey Karmant! Did you ever slog so hard when you were in that dingy office of yours?" Arun needled him. The others greeted his sarcasm with peals of loud laughter.

Karmant's composure never wavered. "Yes, I did. But I'm sad to say, I've realized that had I maintained a calm composure and effective team-building communication, perhaps I would have been able to achieve better results from all that work."

His answer silenced the team. Not even a paper rustled in the stillness of the room.

Arun tried again. "You were a jerk when you sat in that seat, did you know that? Ask us what we felt. You were like a snake that hissed at us and terrified everyone, whenever we tried to open our mouths! You are a pathetic and ruthless person, SIR!"

Karmant could feel his blood warming up and shooting into his eyes. He could even feel the heat in his ears. But with the genie on his mind, and dedicated to his intended practice for the day, he counted upward from 1 to 100 as his coworkers watched him in suspense! 1... 2... 3... 4... 5... 6... 7... 8...

As part of his mind counted the numbers, another part marveled. "I can't believe this; I can count the numbers this time… Oh Genie, thank you so much. Your tips are working. You have saved me from causing yet another disaster. I wish I could talk to you right away. You will be so happy after hearing this… Now, I understand giving in to anger is like putting fuel into a fire. If I want to extinguish the fire of bitterness among these people, I need to show love to them. As difficult as it will be to start, without that I won't receive love from them."

He mustered his courage. "Yes. I regret my rude behavior. I should have known better. Now I understand what words filled with rage can do to a person… I am experiencing that now… Forgive me!" With a sudden jerk, he walked away from his seat. Everyone was dumbfounded and gazed after him.

"Is he okay?"

"Is he undergoing some psychiatric treatment, or going to therapy, or something?"

Arun still scoffed. "He simply wants to regain his position, guys! That's it. Let's get back to work."

But this time another co-worker, Ravi, chided him. "No. There's been some sort of drastic change in Karmant. The look in his eyes was different. He was trying to take charge of his temper and remain calm…"

Arun shook his head, though his sardonic grin had slipped somewhat. "Oh okay, okay! Let's get back to work. We will get to see more of him."

While walking towards the open terrace, Karmant remembered about forgiveness. The names and faces of people whom he had treated poorly raced through his mind. He mentally imagined all of them in turn and sought forgiveness from each. After a few minutes he felt some relief.

Standing towards the end of the terrace railing, he breathed the fresh air. As he glanced down from the 11th floor at the specks of cars below, his thoughts worked creatively. The cars seemed so tiny from here… but from the ground, even the most compact car looks large. He said to himself, "Troublesome events in our lives are just like these cars. The closer we get to them, the bigger they look to us. It's better to see them from an indifferent detached viewpoint, so they can always remain small."

9

The sky was turning from blue to pink as the sun neared the horizon. As the pleasant rays of sunset enveloped the cityscape, Karmant's face beamed. He felt a divine calmness soothe his nerves and his mind. It signaled to him that it was time to call it a day.

Winning over anger, and holding back his impulse to shoot back with his words, had turned out to be an immense conquest for Karmant today; definitely something to be merry about. Through his own experience he could feel the truth of what the genie had said about taking the remote control of his life into his own hands.

He entered home with lighter footsteps and a lighter heart, and headed straight to the kitchen to greet Bhavana.

"Hi Dear! How are you, and how's little Raju?"

Startled by his voice, she dropped a dish. She looked into his face, dazed, her mind whirling with questions. "What's wrong with him? How come he reached home so early today? Is everything all right?" Little Raju was confused to see a smile on his father's face. They couldn't believe it was for real. With bated breath, all that Bhavana could manage was a small sound, expressing "Fine."

Noticing their expressions, Karmant let a small giggle escape. He politely asked, "Bhavana, I will be in my study for some time. May I take my dinner there?" Without waiting for her reply, he quietly walked toward his room.

Bhavana steadied herself on the table, thinking, "PLEASE… Oh my GOD… Is he okay?… He seems to be some different Karmant…"

She recovered her voice. "Ah, yes, yes… I… I'll do that." With a broad smile, joy infusing her entire existence, she moved swiftly to get his plate ready, thinking, "Oh, I still can't believe it!"

After Bhavana and Raju had retired to bed, Karmant waited for them to fall asleep and then moved swiftly and silently out of the house.

With stars peeking down at Earth from their cold night blanket, Karmant headed for the sandy beach. He was eager to update the genie about his victory over anger. He meditated again on the rock, and was better off than the previous day. The genie arrived with a serene smile.

Before Karmant could speak, the genie greeted him, "Hello, Karmant! Looks like you have won a battle today. I see you in a victorious, and confident mood. I love to see you doing so well."

Karmant was taken aback. "How come the genie knows about my victory? As some stories suggest, can genies be omnipresent?"

He replied, "Yes. It's all because of you! Thanks a lot! I could keep a check on my anger today, and I improved my communication with the team multi-fold. It feels so rejuvenating to be like this. It looks like I'll soon be friends with everyone in the team."

The genie held up a hand in a calming gesture. "Aha… Okay. But let me tell you something. Today you had firmly resolved to practice. So, you were able to accomplish your goal easily, by keeping your intention consistently at the back of your mind. But this shouldn't last for only a day or two; you must practice this for the rest of your life. At all times, you should be consciously aware of the words that you use. Your new outlook and determination of practice should not be affected by your promotion, either."

"Yes, Genie! I will… I promise. Today my colleagues tried to rile me, but I could maintain my cool by counting upward. I even surprised myself when I could respond to them politely! They must have been shocked by my courteous response. I could see a mix of expressions on their faces: some were perplexed, others were surprised. I was wondering how they reacted after I left. Do they believe me, or do they wonder if I'm playing games? After being successful today, I am keen to learn different kinds of model responses for every situation."

The genie nodded. "Okay. Let's do it differently this time. Let me see how much you comprehend by yourself, and I'll fill in the gaps. I will narrate some illustrative dialogues to you, and for every response that I relate, you can tell me the nature of that response. If you get it right, I will train you further. Okay?"

"Okay. I am ready," exclaimed Karmant, full of excitement. He felt like he was seated in the hot seat of a premiere quiz show on a popular TV channel with a nationwide broadcast.

10

Now, it was Karmant's turn.

The genie began: "A child was raising funds for a project. When he asked a miserly person for funds, he replied, 'First focus on your studies and then do all these rubbish activities.' The child promptly and harshly responded, 'I have asked for money, not your advice.' What kind of a response is this?"

"It is an impolite, angry response."

"Right! Quick and impulsive is the first type of response. People who respond quickly without giving a second thought to their opinion often tend to respond in the same acerbic manner everywhere, in all situations. Just like the child, they quickly retaliate against whatever they are told. For such people, humbly accepting someone's advice is farfetched!"

"I see. When I was in crisis, nobody came to my rescue. I resented them at the time; but in hindsight, I realize that it could have been because of my past rash behavior towards them. I can relate to the child. I am eager to know about better ways to respond."

"Karmant, it's good that you are able to scrutinize your life using this knowledge. Having understood the downside of this response, it's equally important to know it has advantages in some situations."

"Does it? I was resolving not to give an impulsive response in any situation. What situations would benefit from an impulsive response?"

"The waking hour, in the morning, is the right time for a quick response; otherwise you will fall asleep again. Whenever you feel like undertaking a new task or a good opportunity, always give a quick response. Otherwise, with the passage of time, your motivation weakens. As the new task is unfamiliar, you may find it difficult to accomplish and take more time to complete it. You may even be tempted to procrastinate on starting it. If you give a quick response you will build momentum, and soon will become efficient in doing that job. You will complete the job and achieve success easily."

"Wow! I would have never thought of these examples. Thank you, Genie, for this valuable guidance!"

"Let's move on to the next type of response. I will give the example, and you identify the response. Ready?"

"Yes, Genie, I'm ready."

"A bald man was passing by a stranger. The stranger mocked him, saying, 'The moon is shining.' The bald man hit him on his head with a stick and said, 'Now see the stars.'"

Karmant laughed loudly. "That was hilarious! The bald man seems to be very aggressive."

"Karmant, you are right. Rash, or aggressive, is the second type of response. The bald man in this example thinks that he has successfully taught the stranger a lesson. What he doesn't know is that the stranger will now be on the lookout for a means to put him down in order to gratify his ego. Either he will try to get the upper hand, or he will try to get even with him. He will curse him in his heart of hearts. You must understand that an aggressive response is like shooting yourself in the foot. In life, never give an aggressive response under any circumstances."

Karmant went quiet. "That's a very good lesson for me. I need to make drastic changes in my behavior." Karmant sat down on a stone, looking dejectedly at the shiny sand. "I feel sorry for my secretary. I would always get angry, give a rude and quick response to whatever she said, and shout at her for the smallest things… even if she was a minute late to arrive at my office. Whenever I was stressed, or sometimes scared about the outcomes of my meetings, I would always respond hastily, without giving a second thought about what I was saying. That's why today I stand as an example of dreadful communication."

The genie's voice was gentle. "I am glad that you understand these things today, Karmant. Because you have become aware of these issues, your communication is now going to recover very soon."

On watching the reflection of the stars shining and dancing in the sea and reflected in the genie's big eyes, Karmant felt motivated again. "Isn't it advantageous to be aggressive if we intend the well-being of the other person? Despite repeatedly telling Raju to get up early for preschool, he fails to do so. At those times I shout at him."

"Karmant, if you are doing it for his well-being, and not out of your own frustration, then in this case your aggressive response is valid."

"Okay. Sometimes, I return home tired and see Raju's toys scattered here and there. I feel frustrated and aggressive looking at that mess, and start shouting at him. In that case, I should be able to tolerate Raju's unorganized behavior, knowing that he is a small child."

"Yes, Karmant. That's the next response we are going to talk about. Let me give you an example.

A housewife screams as if she has witnessed a gruesome murder, but it turns out she has only seen a tiny cockroach. Tell me, what is the appropriate response in this case?"

"I think she is doing it out of fear. But still, instead of responding in such an exaggerated manner, she could have been more patient."

"Good guess, Karmant. Patient and analytical is the third type of response. The fruit of patience is not only sweet, but also health-enhancing. Many people respond impatiently when faced with pain, suffering, or fear. They can't tolerate even a little pain and start shouting. They become impatient even in trivial discussions, and raise their voice to force their views upon people. They need to pause before responding. By not giving a patient response, they become patients."

Karmant heartily laughed at the joke.

The genie continued, "Sometimes, however, people give a patient and analytical response at the wrong time, which causes delays in their work."

"I can relate to that very well. Sometimes I procrastinate responding to client messages thinking that I will give them due attention later. As a result, there would be delayed response to their problems on my side, which sometimes also led to miscommunication."

"Yes, you got it right, Karmant."

"I think that, in retrospect, I was wrong to react impulsively and angrily when I was engulfed by negative thoughts. I should have observed patience."

"Good retrospection, Karmant! You can practice patient response in everyday life situations; even something as simple as ringing a doorbell. Suppose you ring the doorbell more than twice and yet nobody answers the door. You lose patience. You start shouting, 'Open the door. Why isn't anyone opening the door?' At such times, keep your cool and wait patiently. Instead of shouting, speak softly. You can also practice patient response when your phone rings. Don't pick up your phone impatiently as soon as it rings; instead, wait until it rings two or three times and pick it up in a calm, peaceful manner. Your patience and endurance will increase with this behavior, and you will be more patient in communicating with others.

Oftentimes lack of patience makes you utter words which make you repent later. Furthermore, when you're impatient you can't keep any secrets and lose your trustworthiness. You need to have control over your speech. When someone mispronounces a word because of a tongue twist, he feels ashamed; but when he uses the same tongue to abuse, lie, and curse or make fun of others, he doesn't feel ashamed. People who are determined to use their tongue with care are always happy.

There is a saying: Wounds caused by a cane or a stone can heal, but the wounds caused by the tongue remain fresh all through life. Keeping this in mind, we should control our tongue and behave humbly through speech."

"This is marvelous, Genie! The way you explain things is just so easy; and it's so applicable to daily life! I have really learned a lot today. It feels so good to know these things and understand them so well. Which response is the next one, now?"

"The fourth type of response is a placative or passive response. This response arises from a state of proactive alertness, rather than reactive sloppiness. To respond in this way, take a step back, observe the situation objectively, and then respond."

"For me, it's natural to react impulsively. I need to be proactively alert in order to respond in this way. Could you please elaborate more on this? I want to understand it better."

"Yes. Always give a passive response when you are grief-stricken. People who advertise their grief end up with more of it. Tell your doctor about your pains and problems, but don't tell everyone. There are many times in life when you have to make decisions where you are bound to suffer no matter what you choose. At such times you must give a passive response. Your response should come after a pause, with humility."

"Okay. Now I understand. When my managing director, Mr. Desai, informed me about my demotion, I was struck with grief. I retaliated with very harsh words, which eventually let depression enter me. If I had passively accepted what had unfolded before me, I wouldn't have suffered so badly."

"That's correct. During troubled times it's wise to respond with patience and courage, without getting unduly excited. But, as in the other situations, it's not the wisest response in every situation. People compulsorily give placative responses when they are faced with conflicting situations. At such times a stronger response is expected from them, but they shrug off their responsibility by remaining inactive. Your response is a signal of your success."

"Okay. I got it. I need to reflect on it. What's the next response?"

"Karmant, due to your eagerness and willingness to work on the lessons that I give you every night, I'll tell you the most supreme way of communication now. Listen to it carefully." With seriousness in his voice and face, the genie looked down at Karmant.

Seeing the stillness of his gaze, Karmant straightened up and looked into his eyes.

"The fifth, and last, type of response is the complete response, which arises from an awakening state. It encompasses the complete way of communicating on earth, through co-operation, love, and joy. This is the way of oneness.

One identical response does not work in all situations. You need to remain aware in that small gap between an event and the corresponding action.

When you fold your four fingers into your palm, you make a fist; this fist signifies the complete response. Mastering the complete response means that you know the way to use all four fingers in harmony. When you need to give a quick response, you will do just that. You will give a passive response where it is required. Where a patient response is needed, you will give one. You will speak aggressively when it is for the good of others. If you can do this, it means that you have understood the complete response.

Just as one needs to dig a well before he is thirsty, one also needs to prepare for all these responses in advance. Let me quiz you on responses."

Karmant felt exhilarated. "That's exciting. I am ready."

The genie began. "When someone praises you, what should be your response?"

"It should be either a silent response or a restrained response."

"When someone makes fun of you, what should be your response?"

"It should be a delayed and a patient response."

"What kind of response should you give when you are in trouble?"

"I should give a patient or a humble response."

"When the phone is ringing and no one is answering it, how should you respond?"

"I should give a patient or a humble response."

"When you are unwell, what kind of response will you give to people?"

"I can give an opposite response, by being happy. I can also give a humble response."

"When you are tired and someone asks you to fetch him some water, or asks for any other aid, how will you respond?"

"I should be quick in action and patient in speech. In responding with generosity I get a chance to stretch my comfort zone, and will even feel happy about helping."

"How should you react when someone is getting angry with you?"

"I should give a silent, a humble, or a patient response."

"When someone doesn't do your work on time, what should be your response?"

"It should be either a patient or an opposite response. I can still happily deal with him as if nothing has happened."

"When someone goes back on his word, how will you respond to him?"

"I could either be patient or give an opposite response. I will forgive him and deal with him as if nothing has happened."

"When another person responds in a wrong manner, how should you react?"

"By giving a silent or an opposite response."

"When someone steals your ideas and calls them his own, what kind of response should you give?"

"I should give a delayed and a patient response."

"What should be your response when your neighbor throws his garbage in front of your house?"

"It should be humble. I can also give an opposite response by forgiving him."

"When your country gets defeated in a cricket match, what kind of response should you give?"

"A delayed and an opposite response."

"What should be your response in case of the death of a relative?"

"It should be silent and restrained."

"What should be your response when you have to do many tasks at a time?"

"Humble in speech and quick in action."

"When you are compared with some other person, what kind of response should you give?"

"I will give an opposite response by being happy instead of being jealous."

"When you are besieged with thoughts of disappointment, what response should you give?"

"A delayed or an opposite response. Instead of indulging in thoughts of disappointment, I will invite thoughts of hope, creativity, and happiness."

"What should your response be when you are scared of something?"

"It should be an opposite response; I should act with bravery."

"What should your response be when you feel like appreciating someone?"

"It should be a quick response."

"What should your response be when someone tries to bribe you?"

"I should give a patient and a firm response."

"What should be your response when feelings of hatred and revenge arise in you?"

"It should be a passive and an opposite response."

"What should be your response when you think of giving charity?"

"It should be a quick response."

"When you get many things to eat at a time, what should your response be?"

"It should be an opposite and a restrained response."

"What should your response be when unexpected guests arrive?"

"It should be a patient and a quick response. I will greet them immediately with hospitality."

"What should your response be in case of a power failure?"

"It should be an opposite and a patient response."

The genie beamed with satisfaction. "Very well answered, Karmant! If you are ready with an appropriate response in all situations, whether trouble-free or difficult, from the smallest to the biggest, then you have begun to know the complete response. When you know the correct way and time to give the correct response, you have then mastered the complete response. The complete response is a supreme response and a supreme way of living. When your actions and communication are equipped with the right understanding, you learn to give the best response. You then, yourself, become the Genie of Communication!"

Karmant looked at the genie and smiled. The genie's eyes shined with exuberance and knowledge. The glimmer in them expressed his feeling of satisfaction for having taught Karmant the entirety of what he wanted him to learn.

Bidding farewell to the stars and to the genie for the night, Karmant slipped into his warm bed. He looked at the stars from his window. He wondered: Is there a special relation that I hold with these stars? Was it his bed that made him feel warm, or were the stars which gleamed far away warmer today? He sent warm thoughts back into the universe: Goodnight, my sparkling friends!

11

Suffused with the warmth of the wisdom of the previous night, Karmant woke up feeling excited and full of love for himself and everyone. Love was seeping into him: into his body, mind, heart, and thoughts. Love shone from his own two gleaming stars… his eyes; they were saying it all today.

"Good morning, Bhavana. So, what's for breakfast today?" asked Karmant lovingly.

"I'm sorry, but I made the usual thing… actually… it's orange juice and egg omelet."

"That's wonderful! A healthy breakfast at the start of the day! Let's have breakfast together."

"Oh! Actually, I was just going to get Raju to the bathroom to get him ready for preschool. But if you insist, I can join you for breakfast. I'll… I'll just come…"

"No, no… It's okay. Just go ahead with your routine, or else you will get delayed. Don't bother, I'll finish quickly and will leave for office. Maybe I'll join you for breakfast a bit earlier tomorrow. Okay?"

"Oh yes… I mean, no… it's okay, I'll change my time tomorrow."

"Bhavana, it's okay. You go ahead. I'll see you soon, when I get back in the evening."

Bhavana was not only petrified, but also speechless. She could not believe the change in him. What had happened? How was he getting better day by day? Something must have definitely come about… Some miracle… Some blessing… She closed her eyes and said, "Thank you, God."

The workday started with a team meeting. Jay walked into the room with a sullen face, radiating tenseness and reeking of cigarette smoke.

With some hitches, he began. "Hello, team. We have tough business to deal with today. I fail to understand why we under performed this quarter. We are falling behind in assuring the quality of all the modules, and our output is not satisfactory. What has been going wrong?"

Another team member, Sunil, retorted, "We are already doing our best. What more do you expect from us?"

Karmant could immediately sense a feeling of hurt and unwillingness to cooperate behind these words. It was an impulsive and aggressive response. Hearing such words spoken by someone other than himself, he realized how destructive words can be when said without thought.

Jay rebuked him harshly. "That's not the right answer, Sunil! Don't you realize that we are running short of time to meet the project deadline?"

Sunil bristled. "Oh stop it! Just because you're the team leader doesn't mean that you're always right! And…"

"Please stop, Sunil," Karmant intervened with a polite tone. "He is not blaming you; only trying to find the cause for the delay. He is obligated to report a reason to the higher authorities and to the client. Please be a little more patient. Let's try to arrive at a solution, together as a team."

Sunil turned on Karmant. "Oh yeah! Since when have you become Mr. Right in this office? What do you understand about patience and teamwork? Do these words even exist in your dictionary, and who are you to teach me? Mind your own business."

"Let's stop this argument, please. It's doing us no good," Karmant interrupted helplessly. "I sincerely apologize to everyone for my behavior in the past. I am trying to communicate better now." He wondered why people were stuck on things of the past.

There was an awkward pause. Then Jay stated, in a tone of authority and agitation, "Allright team, let's conclude this meeting. Please get back to work, and start putting in extra time towards your targets. I want the deadlines to be met at any cost."

The team members whispered amongst themselves for some time, and then dispersed. Karmant was the last one to leave. Looking back, he saw Jay slump in the chair and lose himself in thoughts. Karmant walked over to him and consoled him, "It's okay. We will be able to do it. Don't worry. Things will turn out well."

Jay was taken aback at his positive outlook. "You seem to have changed quite a lot, Karmant. Thank you for understanding what I meant then. I am worried about the client. He is a new client, and we need to apprise him of our progress tomorrow. You know how these client meetings are. In this period of economic depression it has become far more important to retain all our clients."

"Don't worry. Just think positively. I'll put in extra effort to get things ready on time. Let me see if together we can manage things before the deadline. Also, I have noticed that this client is of a very analytical bent of mind. If you are patient and polite while giving him all the data during the call, he should understand."

"Thanks a lot, Karmant. Your words really motivate me."

Karmant felt a wave of happiness sweep over him. He had, for the first time, communicated well and helped someone through the use of his words. He finally understood the healing effect that words can have if spoken correctly.

As he walked towards the door, in high spirits, Jay called after him. "Hey Karmant! Would you like to accompany me to the client meeting tomorrow? Your past experience in handling client meetings will be handy."

"Of course, I'll be there tomorrow," exclaimed Karmant. He felt joyful like never before. He was not sure if it was the appreciation from Jay, or being invited to the client meeting, or his own learning; but it was all because of the wonders of right communication and building confidence in his ability. What miracles words can create!

For the rest of the day, he worked better and quicker than ever before. He was happy and motivated, and was eagerly awaiting the client meeting that was to come the next day.

12

Winding up his work, Karmant stretched his tense back and shoulders and left for home. It had been a hard day indeed. At home he spent time with Bhavana and his son. Raju was busy, drawing and coloring a rainbow.

Karmant thought to himself, "Life is truly a rainbow: colorful. Every event brings with it some new color… some new lesson…"

After some time, he excused himself to resume his office work at home. He quickly placed a gentle kiss on Raju's soft cheek and winked goodnight to Bhavana. Watching them smile made him feel blissful. Smiles… Rainbow… A beautiful life indeed…

Bhavana was beginning to accept the new Karmant. Her happiness knew no bounds. She thought, "I wish he spent some more time with us… But I'm happy." She tucked Raju into bed beside her and peeked out of the window. She looked at the always-twinkling stars and thanked them. May this twinkle always continue in my life, she prayed. The stars twinkled and smiled back at her.

Karmant was deeply engrossed in his work at the computer. One by one, he completed as many files as he could to allow his team to achieve the target. He wanted to show everyone that he too could work hard and contribute towards team performance. His new-found focus and drive gave him deep satisfaction.

Time passed, and the night grew darker. Karmant became so immersed in his work that he completely forgot about the genie. Dozing off at the table, he dreamt of the genie and woke up with a jerk. He immediately sat in meditation, and called out for the genie.

The genie arrived, the room somehow containing his great size. "Hello, Karmant! Where have you been? We haven't finished the lessons yet!"

"Oh, Genie! I'm so sorry. It's just that I was held up with work today. Can you believe it, I dozed off and dreamt of you! That's how I was reminded of you, and I immediately got up."

The genie smiled, and with a wise and calm voice explained, "Many a time, help arises in dreams, or through some words we hear, or some book suddenly placed in our hands, or even a movie given as a gift by a friend. These words or items may seem to relate to nothing specific, but they are messages for us. Dreams are one medium through which the wiser forces of nature help you to recollect and decode the messages you receive."

"Really? Wow! That's amazing. I have never paid any close attention to any of that," exclaimed Karmant.

"Well, since you are working at home at this hour, can I presume that you are getting involved with your team and have started enjoying your work?"

"Yes! I love the work now. I have realized the importance of teamwork: it's the only way that the manager can meet his deadlines. It's a real pity if the manager can't communicate properly with his team that works for him so hard, day and night."

"Well, but everyone works to earn a living," the genie commented, quizzically.

"Yes, but when there is a friendly, motivated atmosphere within the team, everybody enjoys performing. They're even willing to take on additional work, if it's required. That's because they love their manager, and want to put in their best, just for him."

"Well, well… That's some philosophical talk; sounds really good. So, now you totally understand the importance of effective communication. I'm glad you are able to practice what you've learned. The more you practice it, the more you will notice that there is a natural expression of love, joy, and peace that occurs in teams. Your loving communication enhances the natural expression that all human beings want."

"Yeah… but I was slightly troubled by an incident that happened today in the office. There was an argument between my manager, Jay, and my colleague, Sunil, during the meeting. It was plainly a misunderstanding. I tried to reconcile them, but Sunil didn't take it well. Instead, he threw my past at me. I apologized to them for my past misdemeanors, but he didn't seem any less bitter. How can I clarify misunderstandings?"

"Karmant, it's good that you were able to apologize to them. Make sure you truly forgive them as well. So, we have a topic ready for us today: misunderstandings.

Conflict is a fact of life; and it is not necessarily bad. Conflicts occur at all levels of interaction: at work, among friends, within families, and between partners. When a conflict occurs, the relationship is either undermined or strengthened. If handled well, conflicts can be productive, leading to deeper understanding, mutual respect, and closeness.

Often people hold each other responsible for misunderstandings. But that's a destructive way of communication.

People adopt a number of different styles to manage conflict. In the first style, a person avoids or denies the existence of any conflict. He doesn't pursue his own concerns or those of the other person, and he doesn't address the conflict. Instead, he sidesteps, postpones, or simply withdraws. The other person may mistake the avoidance for agreement. This style can be appropriate, when the issue is trivial. Unfortunately, when no discussion takes place, people hesitate to look within and weigh the feelings the conflict instilled in them, and thus the conflict lingers in the background. Every further interaction with the same person stimulates that feeling and draws conflict out, leading to strained relationships. It doesn't serve any good for the common goal.

In the second style of managing conflict, one firmly pursues his concerns despite the resistance of the other person. He gets furious and blames the other person in order to force his views upon him. If the other person reacts in kind the argument rages on, in time resulting in increased abuse. This stance does nothing to resolve the conflict, and furthermore causes more pain and hurt to all involved. It does nothing to bring about any possibility of co-operation, empathy, or respect for the other person's opinion. It serves no purpose at all.

In the third way of managing conflict, one resolves the conflict by playing games with power and influence. He tries to belittle the other person by using worthiness and power as leverage. He acts in an aggressive way in order to achieve his goals, without seeking co-operation from the other person, or at the expense of the other person's viewpoint. He treats the argument like a competition, and fails to understand that this is a never-ending race; the loser will search for an opportunity to get even with him. Even with all these negative ramifications, this style may be appropriate for emergencies where time is of the essence. It can be used as a last resort to resolve a long-lasting conflict."

"What are the good ways of handling conflict? What are the best ways to communicate during conflict?" asked Karmant.

"Conflicts range from being minor, unimportant differences, to disagreements which can threaten the survival of relationships. Conflicts can be easily maneuvered and overcome if both participants view the conflict as a disagreement to be solved mutually. This perspective helps each to take responsibility for the solution, and to build that solution with the consensus of both of them. Furthermore, it helps by building a platform to resolve any future conflicts. Each will know what can generate crisis between them, and how to resolve such a crisis. Though easy to understand, this principle is often put off until it's too late. Thus, special care must be taken to establish rules before any conflict takes shape. This is known as platform-creation. This is a collaborative style of conflict management which leads to a win-win outcome.

Many times, because of immediate personal interests, one may not actively participate in the course of conflict resolution. Primarily, listening and considering the opinion of an opponent help to resolve 99% of a conflict. Many conflicts are caused by verbal miscommunication, or lack of communication. Such superficial conflicts are hollow within and hold no damaging intentions. Thus, simply surrendering to the conflict will make matters worse, curbing the freedom in a relationship. It is imperative that both parties remain honest. They should be open to explore the possibilities of problem solving, and to search deeper for reasons if conflicts happen regularly."

"How can we prevent these conflicts and misunderstandings? Can't we get rid of them altogether?" asked Karmant, thinking deeply over what the genie had already said.

"By nature, most people are not interested in creating any conflict. But problems occur when we fail to use co-operative approaches and consistent, amiable words in our dealing with others. It is always in our interest to have good, flexible, progressive relationships with everyone. Most of the time conflict arises when we fail to establish a co-operative platform with others.

We seldom create conflict intentionally. Instead, we are unaware of the way our communication and behavior contributes to interpersonal problems. Tiredness, insufficient sleep, hunger, or our compulsion to fall back to our usual style of response can create an urge to fulfill our desires without considering others' viewpoints. As a result, we find ourselves in conflicting situations.

In order to prevent conflict, it is important to realize where we go wrong and change our style. Think about ways where you can improve your tone and reactions. Work on it consistently, every day, and soon you will be able to change your usual style of communication. In the end, evaluate yourself. Did you succeed? In which situations did you succumb? While it could be the other person who created the conflict, your response lies in your hands. You have the choice to control or to change."

"Right! It takes two hands to clap… likewise, any argument or difference of opinion requires two people who disagree."

"Exactly! So, it's important to learn to communicate effectively to reduce conflicts. When your views clash with someone else's, detach yourself emotionally from the situation. Then you and the other person can deal with your differences on a rational level in order to resolve the conflict. Here are some ways to do this:

Diffuse anger: When someone comes at you, armed with a series of arguments and reasons to blame you for his anger, simply take responsibility. This means that you do nothing but simply agree with the person. When you agree with his point of view, it gets difficult for him to keep up his rage. For example, 'I should have given you time last night, as promised. You are absolutely right. I wish I could be more responsible.' This could feel unfair to you; but not completely, as there is always some truth in what the other person says. We must know that every person has his own way of perceiving things. Agreeing with them doesn't imply that we are compromising our guiding principles. We simply validate the other person's bearing so that we can move on to a healthier platform of discussion and resolution. This may be hard to practice, but by nature human beings are well-equipped with inner strength and the ability to delay reactions in order to achieve positive results. Sometimes we have to lose at first in order to ultimately win.

Place yourself in their shoes: Showing compassion for the other person makes him feel important and heard. It is an important listening technique. Empathy can be practiced at the level of thought or of feeling. To practice empathy at the thought level, try to show that you have understood what the other person is trying to say. You can reiterate what the other person wants to say in your own words, such as, 'I think you are saying that you have lost trust in me.' To practice empathy at the feeling level, first accept the feelings of the other person. Never assume another's state of mind before you listen to how they actually feel. When you listen, make no judgment. Don't attribute nonexistent emotions to his words; such as, 'You're confused by your emotions right now.' Rather, indicate your view through words which show empathy, as well as which convey no direct verdict. Acknowledge how the other person probably feels. It is better to clarify your assumption than rendering it as a direct statement. For example, 'I guess you are probably feeling very bad and seem to be pretty mad at me right now.'

Ask gentle, probing questions, to know how and what the other person is thinking and feeling. Encourage him to talk fully and explain all that is on his mind. For example, 'Do you wish to share anything else with me?'

Take responsibility for your feelings: Instead of placing blame on the other person for making you feel a certain way, take responsibility for your own feelings. Feeling sad or happy is in your hands and no one can make you feel happy or sad unless you consent. Understanding this principle will reduce your defensiveness and will help in creating a common platform. For example, it is much more effective to say, 'I feel upset that this thing has come between us,' than to say, 'You are the one who has brought this unhappiness.'

Show respect: Say positive things about the other person, even if the other person is angry with you. For example, 'I genuinely respect you for bringing this issue up. I admire your strength and your caring attitude.'"

The genie paused to make sure Karmant was following his words and taking in all he had said.

"Karmant, these techniques can surely help to minimize misunderstandings. However, only when you truly forgive the other person can a conflict be managed successfully. With true forgiveness you will have a clean slate, a clean state of mind. You can then deal with the other person harmoniously, without having any grudges from the past. Tell me, how do you feel about Sunil now?"

"Although I apologized to him, I still feel hurt by his rash response."

"The hurt feeling indicates that you have not truly sought forgiveness from him."

"How can I do that? Can you help me?"

"Karmant, I have already explained how to practice forgiveness. If you practice forgiveness immediately after a hurtful event, or at least before you go to sleep, you will be relieved of these negative feelings. Let's practice it now.

Close your eyes, and mentally recall Sunil's image. Seek forgiveness from him from the bottom of your heart by saying in your mind,

'Dear Sunil,

I seek forgiveness from you.

Please forgive me for the hurt I caused you

through my words, actions, feelings, or thoughts.

I will ensure that I don't commit such a mistake again.'

Forgive him for his misbehavior as well, by saying,

'Dear Sunil,

I forgive you for the hurt you caused me

through your words, actions, feelings, or thoughts.'

Let go of the grudges against Sunil by saying,

'Dear Sunil,

> *I am letting go of the hatred, resentment or complaint that I have held in my mind against you.*
>
> *I forgive you. I love you. I respect you.*
>
> *I seek forgiveness for carrying a grudge against you.*
>
> *Please forgive me.'*

Now, slowly open your eyes. How do you feel now?"

Karmant sat quietly for a moment before speaking. "I am feeling relieved now. I am really grateful to you for teaching me these miraculous ways of overcoming negativity. I'm sure that if either of these techniques had been used today, there would have been no argument at all! I wish I had learned all of these techniques before being demoted!" Karmant said sadly.

"But then you were to learn it this way, Karmant. Your demotion has been a blessing in disguise, because it kindled the serious need within you to learn these lessons. Otherwise, you wouldn't have absorbed this understanding so deeply."

"Yes, you are right. Earlier I used to take everything for granted. I also took the results of my communication for granted, without ever thinking of how people in my team actually felt. There is an old saying by Bernard Shaw which I remember: The problem with communication is the illusion that it has occurred."

"Don't worry, Karmant. You are too good to be kept at the position that you are at now. You will rise back again."

"I hope so. There is a client meeting that I have to attend the day after tomorrow. I really hope I perform well."

"Rest assured, Karmant. It's been a long lesson for tonight. I'll see you again tomorrow. Goodnight!"

The genie bade him farewell for the night and went back to the unknown and unseen, yet existing realms contained somewhere in the vast space of the universe.

Karmant looked into the emptiness of the night wistfully. "Ah Genie… I wish I were able to lead a carefree life like you…"

"Positive self-talk, Karmant," echoed the voice of the genie, reminding Karmant to keep building motivation and positivity.

Karmant looked up into the sky in search of the voice, but only saw the stars, his new friends. How do they always manage to remain happy and shine with joy, everlastingly…?

13

The next day seemed overly busy for everyone at the office. Jay stopped by at Karmant's desk and chirruped, "Hi! How are you doing?"

"Oh! You really startled me. I'm doing well. I was working from home yesterday, and have put a copy of the draft on your desk. Did you get a chance to go through it?"

"Yes, Karmant; I reviewed it this morning. It's looking good. You've indeed done well to complete a major milestone of the project. However, overall, we are still lagging behind on the delivery milestones. Could you please quickly join me in the meeting room? Mr. Desai is waiting for us."

"What!? Say that again… Mr. Desai… Are you sure…?"

"Oh, c'mon Karmant. Let's go."

Karmant swiftly got up from his seat and kept pace with Jay to the meeting room.

"Okay. Listen, Karmant. I have informed Mr. Desai about the proposed client meeting. He wants to validate my decision of including you in the meeting."

"Are you serious? I mean… He will never agree to this decision…" said

Karmant as they entered the meeting room.

They were signaled to sit down in the huge, black executive chairs. There was a long pause.

Mr. Desai broke the silence, "Good Morning, Karmant."

"Good morning, Mr. Desai. How are you?"

"I am well, thank you, Karmant. I have called for this discussion to plan our approach for tomorrow's checkpoint meeting with Kevin, our client representative. We will be apprising him of the progress that our Quality Assurance team has made on the project. As you may already be aware, Kevin is the center head for our client. Being a single point of contact, he tracks the progress of all the projects to ensure their timely completion. This is one of our prestigious clients. We have bagged this business with great effort, thanks to our chairman's personal connection."

He relaxed into his chair with his fingers revolving over the round pen holder kept at the desk; his gaze fixed on Karmant.

Karmant was almost gasping, his throat constricted and parched with nerves, but was determined to look calm. The thought came to his mind: silence was the best answer. He remained silent.

After few seconds, Mr. Desai broke the uncomfortable silence. "So, what do you think, Karmant?"

"About what?" questioned Karmant, his voice cracking.

"Oh, the client, and the fact that Jay wants you to assist him at the meeting tomorrow."

"Yes, Mr. Desai, I will be there in the meeting tomorrow."

"And do what?"

"Talk to them about the project."

"Talk what about the project?"

Karmant felt the words aimed at him like a bullet.

"I am aware of the deadlines and the possible delays."

"Hmm. Go on…"

Karmant sensed that Mr. Desai had stopped playing with the pen holder and was now playing with him instead. His posture was stiff and his eyes bored into Karmant's. Mr. Desai didn't have confidence in Karmant's ability to engage with the client at such a high profile meeting; that was evident. The meeting was indeed sensitive, and was going to require patience… Patience… Yes, that was the answer!

Karmant's voice steadied. "Since there is a delay on our side, we can patiently explain to him the reason for the delay, and then…"

"Did you just mention patience, Karmant?"

"Yes, Mr. Desai. Is anything wrong?"

"No. Go on. What reasons are you going to give?"

"We can request him to extend the timeline, and assure him we will adhere to it. Besides owning up to the fact that a few key resources have quit, we can also point out how the sense of turmoil and insecurity that our employees are experiencing due to the wave of economic recession is impacting their performance at work. This is indeed the reason why we are having delays on our projects. We can frankly share this with Kevin and explain the real issues. I am sure he will understand. We can always point out that our quality numbers are still looking good. If we give all the data in a professional manner, I am sure he will accept this one-time delay without worrying about it becoming a habit."

"How did you come to this conclusion?"

"I think that's the best explanation we can give. In fact, the recession stress is a reality almost everywhere."

"Okay." Mr. Desai looked at him intently for a long moment, thinking. The silence was killing Karmant. He thought: I hope I haven't created any mess…

Mr. Desai was still looking at the round pen holder in his stiff hands. Suddenly, he got up and left the office, signaling Jay to meet him outside. As Jay trotted after Mr. Desai, he signaled for Karmant to meet him later.

Karmant profusely gulped in air. He was restless, anxiously awaiting the outcome.

14

Karmant continued working at his desk, but his mind was in turmoil waiting for the news. He felt as if time were crawling. As the clock ticked to 12 o'clock and disappointment was settling into him, he remembered the acceptance mantra: "Can I accept this uncomfortable situation?" He felt a little bit relieved. After some time he repeated the mantra again. This time, he found he could completely accept the situation. He thanked the genie from the bottom of his heart and patiently resumed his work. At 6 o'clock in the evening he decided to call it a day.

As he breezed out of the office, he nearly bumped into Jay. Jay teased him, "Hey Karmant, hang in there. I have some news!"

"What's the news?" Karmant asked apprehensively, holding his breath.

Jay patted him on his shoulder. "Relax, Karmant. Nothing to worry about! Mr. Desai has agreed that you should join the meeting tomorrow. So, be in meeting room number five at 10 AM sharp."

Karmant's happiness knew no bounds. Somehow he managed to speak. "Ohh… Yes… Sure… I will be there."

"Okay, Karmant. See you tomorrow. Bye for now."

As Jay left, Karmant turned towards the parking lot. Meeting room number five triggered his past memories. He remembered his last meeting with Mr. Malhotra, and the announcement of his demotion. This time meeting room number five will give me some good news, he thought… But how do I prepare myself for the meeting? I have to get back to the genie tonight.

All through the commute, and even after reaching home, he ruminated about the meeting. When Bhavana welcomed him, he was lost in thoughts. With a caressing look, she asked, "Hi Karmant! What's the matter? You seem tense. Is everything alright?" He gently responded, "I am alright. Don't worry." He gulped down his food like a starving man and waited for Bhavana and Raju to go to bed, continuing to think about the meeting.

When they bade him goodnight he rushed towards the beach. He sat in meditation, but the onslaught of his thoughts wouldn't allow him to catch hold of them and number them. He tried to intensify his concentration, but his impatience made him check for the arrival of the genie intermittently. Finding the genie still absent, Karmant worked hard, breathed deeply, and meditated well. This helped him calm his turbulent thoughts and regain his composure. The genie arrived silently and watched him meditate. On the count of twenty, Karmant slowly opened his eyes and found the genie right in front of him. It was a pleasure to see him after refreshing meditation. He felt elated.

"Hello, Karmant! You are doing better in your meditation with each day. This state will help you at all times and in all realms of the universe, and allow you to access the peace within you. What's the reason for this hurry? You called out for me really soon today. Is everything well?"

"Yes, Genie. All is wonderful. Some great opportunities are knocking at my door, and it's all because of you. Thank you for being in my life. I love you," he said in a choked voice, and held the genie's hands. As tears started flowing, he closed his eyes. The genie allowed him to release his feelings. For sometime both were quiet.

Karmant felt deeply connected with the genie. He lost sense of his surroundings. He found the experience not just delightful, but very soulful. He felt full of love and positive energy, more profound and fulfilling than the feelings of his everyday life. He felt as if the genie was reciprocating his feeling of gratitude in silence. After some time, he opened his eyes. Now he felt light and receptive. He experienced joy like he had never experienced before.

The genie sensed his feelings and told him, "This is called bliss, my dear. It surpasses the happiness that comes from external reasons. Once you taste bliss, you will seldom go after fleeting pleasures."

Karmant nodded his head in agreement. "Yes, I understand. I felt happy at being considered for participation in tomorrow's client meeting, but the grateful bliss I felt now is a different kind of happiness. I wish I could always revel in this blissful feeling."

Karmant sighed. "I want to do well in tomorrow's meeting, but the fishy look of our director, Mr. Desai, is really bugging me. In our meeting today, he looked stiff and apprehensive at the idea of me joining in the meeting."

"Non-verbal communication is one of the biggest areas to explore in the field of communication. Your body language speaks volumes about you; even more than your words. Remember, 'It's what you don't say that counts.' In short, body language is a kind of non-verbal communication, where thoughts, intentions, or feelings are expressed by physical behaviors, such as facial expressions, posture, gestures, eye movement, touch, and the use of space. That's why people in the United States and Europe have dedicated classes to teach etiquette. The way you should sit… stand on a stage… your posture while giving a presentation… out in public… dining, and so much more… All of this is essentially known as non-verbal communication."

"Could you tell me how to know what a client may be thinking by his body language?"

"Aha... That is something which I cannot give you, Karmant: the power of reading thoughts."

"Ohh no! It's just that if it were possible for me to sense other people's thoughts while in a meeting, it would have really helped me at this juncture."

The genie smiled and exclaimed, "Your wish is my command! For your latter request, I have an idea! Let's proceed."

Without warning, Swishhh...

"Oh! What's this! Where are we heading? Why couldn't you inform me before lifting me in the air like this? Oh my GOD... I will have a heart attack... I'm so high up, if I fall..."

"Relax, Karmant! I'm holding you tight. You won't have a heart attack, I assure you!" the genie laughed at Karmant's plight. "Let's conduct this lesson in a different way tonight. I am taking you to the United States. You will be able to learn about non-verbal communication there."

"But why the United States!? Why not here!?"

"It's night here! Everyone's asleep. It's daytime in United States, so let's go there. I'll use my powers to make you invisible throughout our journey. We can stop at some good places to learn tonight's lessons. It'll be fun, I promise you, Karmant."

"Okay... okay... Let's be there quickly. I want to get off your shoulder as soon as possible."

With noon at its peak, the bright daylight pierced Karmant's eyes. He rubbed them several times to get a good view. The United States! He couldn't believe he was there! Suspended high above, he could see bustling streets and speeding cars. The movement looked so fast paced from above. He thought to himself, "Indeed, this is a developed country."

Swooping down to alight on the balcony of a big office, the genie took Karmant off his shoulder. Together they walked into the office.

"Why this office?" Karmant whispered.

"Because this company is one of the biggest I.T. giants in the world."

"What!? Are you telling the truth? I don't believe this... I mean... we are in the biggest company in the United States!? Oh my God... this is so thrilling..." Karmant was shaking with excitement.

"Okay, Karmant, listen to me patiently. Let's take a look at an ongoing meeting. I have triggered some subtle powers within you which will enable you to know the thoughts of the participants. With this knowledge, you will be able to correlate their thoughts with their body language. Also, since you are invisible, you won't bother anyone. So, get ready to learn a great lesson for your meeting tomorrow!"

"Am I really invisible? How did this happen?" Karmant questioned the genie, brimming with enthusiasm.

"Karmant, you are forgetting that I am a genie. I belong to a different realm. I can make things possible with permission from the Supreme. Let's concentrate on the conversations now."

They silently moved into a meeting room. Three people were seated around a table. A big screen at the head of the room was displaying a graph that showed a downward slant indicating a fall in sales. Clearly the folks were facing some problem with the sales figures at the company. Karmant leaned in eagerly.

"John, we couldn't meet these projected sales figures for the last year. There were several reasons. There was a downtime error that we were facing, and..." Karmant could hear the thoughts of the men at the table as clearly as the presenter's voice.

> *What's this crap he's saying? He's always full of excuses!*

Soon Karmant started connecting the body language and the thoughts in the minds of the people seated there.

"So, why didn't you predict this and get the I.T. team to take the necessary corrective actions?" asked the guy again, with his hands folded across his stomach and his eyes protruding with a questioning look.

He is going to blame the I.T. guys now, just see. He's such a liar.

"John, it's not our fault. It's the fault of the I.T. guys. They weren't fast enough to manage the problem," he said, standing with palms helplessly opened up.

The boss shut his fist tightly and walked out of the room.

This old fool never believes me! I'm tired of explaining things.

There is no use getting into an argument. He needs to be fired.

Karmant was transfixed, his mind racing. Oh my God... Is this what Mr. Desai felt when he walked out of the room? Oh no... I have to work hard for tomorrow... I must succeed...

The genie's voice finally cut through his thoughts. "Karmant, can we go back now? The meeting is over."

15

"Oh no, Genie! That was such a short meeting. Could we watch one more meeting?"

"Sure! Your wish is my command! We can join in another meeting downstairs, where a salesperson is all ready to present his product. Let's go there."

"Okay. I am not sure how a product presentation will help me, but let's give it a try."

They sneaked into the new meeting room, where the salesman was just opening his heavy briefcase.

"Good morning, Sir. I am from Global Networks. Let me introduce you to our new product in the financial domain," said the salesman in a nervous voice.

I hope I bag this client today. Otherwise I will be sacked.

"Please sit down," the client said in a disinterested, stern tone.

Another boring presentation!

"John, before I begin, I wanted to let you know that I am keenly aware of the fact that your time is very valuable. I am quite grateful that you have still found the time to attend this review meeting," said the marketing fellow politely.

"Please go ahead," John responded, as a smile appeared on his face. The smile looked definitely genuine.

"Looks like the appreciation has worked!" the genie commented, smiling at Karmant.

"Yes…" said Karmant, paying close attention to their body language, dialogue, and thoughts.

"John, our product is the best in the financial domain and comes well recommended. The financial domain, as you know…"

John was frowning and looking down at the table.

I think I'll skip this information. He looks disinterested.

"So let's cut to the chase…"

John sighed and looked up.

Thank God. Looks like he understood.

"More than 70% of all projects in our domain are either delayed or are over budget. The problem boils down to one thing: estimation. Would you agree, John?"

"Sure, I agree. No one can fault what you just said. But what's the solution?"

"That's what I am coming to. Through more than 500 work-days of research we have perfected an estimation model for large financial projects and have coded that algorithm into our latest Project Management Product. It meticulously asks the right questions and helps teams come up with an accurate estimate, and then further helps them easily track the actuals against the estimates. If you present it to your higher ups or to your clients, they will eat out of your hands. I promise you that," said the salesman, with twinkle in his eyes and a confident smile on his lips.

"Ah... the stars are in his eyes... I'm sure he will bag this project," thought Karmant.

This sounds good.
I do have to make a good impression before the annual bonus is due.

"Well... okay... This really sounds good. Will you quickly demo it for me?" asked John, sitting upright in his chair.

"Sure, John," said the salesman, connecting his laptop.

Well, all looks good. He is interested!

"Okay, John. Here we go. This is the main menu page. When you run these templates..." he opened several templates and started pointing out each one's distinguishing factors.

His eyes are not where I am pointing.
Looks like I need to change my focus.

"So John, tell me some of your estimation challenges?"

John responded, watching the clock, "It is mainly that everything is a finger in the air. We are just basing all our estimates on gut feel."

"Okay. Here are some industry benchmarks for effort estimates for the domain you are in. You can select multiple criteria and the benchmarks will change," smiled the sales person confidently.

Hmm, looks good. That was slick.
If it can really do what it says, we should buy this product.

"I think your product looks promising, and I can guide you to the contact person in vendor management. Send them your proposal. I'll make sure we get back to you in a week's time."

"Excellent. Again, thank you for your time. And don't let me hold you back from the Lakers game. It will take you a good 90 minutes to get to the game; and with L.A. traffic, you never know."

"That's true. Good seeing you."

The meeting ended on a positive note.

"So, shall we get back?" asked Karmant with a big smile on his face.

"Aha… You look happy! Let's go!" the genie answered.

They swept back into the air, whisking through fluffy clouds under big stars. Karmant felt like he was one of them today: so close to them, so close to their twinkling; the twinkle of success.

"Thank you, Genie. You have helped me greatly. I am so happy today. I am sure I will perform well in the client meeting tomorrow."

"I wish you all the best, Karmant. Goodnight!"

Preparing for sleep, Karmant slipped into a dreamland of success. He was sure of the sparkle that would return to his life tomorrow. He tasted the glory of success and slept deeply.

16

"Good morning, dear!" exclaimed Karmant, with thrill in his voice.

Bhavana was taken by surprise by his words. She saw Karmant brimming with enthusiasm. She exclaimed, "Good morning! Breakfast is ready."

"I won't have breakfast today," Karmant said, picking up his briefcase. He adjusted his tie and started towards the door. He was eagerly looking forward to the client meeting. He wanted to practice all that he had learned from the genie.

"Why… I mean, I'm sorry to ask… I thought we were going to have breakfast together today… but yeah, okay, go ahead… it should be fine with me…" said Bhavana with slight dismay and anxiety in her voice.

"Look, Bhavana…"

"Oh no… I just thought you would be hungry… really, I'm sorry… I know how angry you get when I stop you on your way out…"

"Bhavana, it's okay. Don't worry. I'm not angry. I have a client meeting today at 10 AM. I think a breakfast will be served there. I'm sorry for not informing you earlier. I wasted your time unnecessarily."

"Oh no! It's okay, Karmant. Don't worry." Bhavana was consoled by his kind words. She felt the joy of being respected. She had been waiting to hear these words from Karmant for a long time. The demonstration that Karmant was concerned about her feelings touched her heart. Her eyes filled with tears.

Karmant continued looking at her. He could grasp what was going on inside her. He thanked the genie for making him sensitive to feelings and words. He realized that words spoken with care can heal someone's longstanding wounds. All these years, his harsh responses had hurt her. He closed his eyes, and from the bottom of his heart, he mentally sought forgiveness from her. "Bhavana, I seek forgiveness from you. Please forgive me for the hurt I caused you through my words, actions, feelings, or thoughts. I will ensure that I don't commit such a mistake again. Thank you for being in my life. I love you." He felt that there was heart to heart communication between him and Bhavana, and that she was also reciprocating.

He said to her, "Thank you for being in my life. I love you."

By now he was feeling light. When he opened his eyes, he saw Bhavana had stopped crying and seemed better. In a choked voice, she said, "I'll be fine. Have a nice day, and all the best for your meeting." Karmant smiled and left. Bhavana felt pleased that life was giving back to her all the old days of love she had missed.

"Good morning, Mr. Desai. May I join you?" asked Karmant before stepping into the meeting room.

"Yes, Karmant. Please come in. Kevin is about to join us. I hope you are prepared." Mr. Desai looked intently at Karmant and Jay.

"Yes, Mr. Desai," smiled Karmant.

"And I'm sure you remember the word, 'patience', that you used yesterday, Karmant?"

"Yes, Sir! I understand. I assure you the meeting will go well."

"Good morning, everyone," a gentleman greeted everyone as he entered the room. Karmant guessed that he must be Kevin. He was at least 6 feet tall and strongly built, and was dressed in a black shirt, a black tie and a black coat. Wow… what a personality, thought Karmant. He looks stern and aggressive… I hope I do well… I can, I am sure."

Filled with confidence, Karmant stood straight and smiled at the new client. He put his hand forward for a handshake and shook hands firmly. The gentleman was pleased.

"Hello, Sir! I am Karmant. It's nice to meet you."

"I'm not sure if I have been introduced to you before…"

"Ah yes," broke in Mr. Desai, "He is one of our senior managers in this company. At present he is working closely with the research team, and is engaged in detailing every aspect of your project. And Karmant, this is Kevin, the client manager for the project that you are working on." Mr. Desai looked at Karmant, hoping that he would respond well.

"We are glad to have you here today, Sir. We really appreciate your time," said Karmant with a welcoming smile.

"Thank you so much, Karmant. And yes… please call me Kevin and not Sir."

"Sure, Sir… I mean Kevin…"

Everyone laughed at the confusion. Mr. Desai was amazed to see Karmant talk with ease. He was happy and felt sure of a positive outcome.

"So gentlemen, what are the backups on accomplishing the deliverables? Why have the project deadlines been delayed?" asked Kevin, with a serious tone.

"Actually, you know the problems the recession has caused…" exclaimed Jay; but he was abruptly interrupted by Kevin.

"C'mon! What does the project deadline have to do with the recession going on now? That can't be an excuse." Kevin gave him a disapproving look.

"No, actually, you're not getting my point here… you should perhaps try to understand from our point of view…" Jay tried to explain with great effort.

Karmant noticed Kevin looking down at the table, shaking his head slightly and not paying attention. He remembered the previous night's lessons on body language and understood that the focus needed to change.

Something signaled from his heart. Do something Karmant… The meeting is turning down a wrong path…

"No, you must understand. We have our commitments back home too. Mr. Desai, why don't you say something?"

Mr. Desai was too uncomfortable to answer, disappointed with the way things had changed course so suddenly and wrongly. He looked helplessly at Karmant.

"Yes, gentlemen, I think Kevin is right. Kevin, I totally agree with you when you say you have commitments back home. But if you could give me a chance, maybe I can explain this better to you," pleaded Karmant with a sincere look at Kevin.

Kevin regarded Karmant sternly. "Yes, please go ahead and convince me I can keep the project here. Otherwise, the project will be leaving the walls of this company… I'm sorry to say that."

"Don't worry, Kevin. More than anything else, you are our most important client. We value your association," exclaimed Karmant.

Kevin looked straight up at Karmant, and looked pleased. "Thank you for your kind words, Karmant."

Everyone breathed a sigh of relief. Now, everyone waited with bated breath to hear Karmant's attempt at convincing Kevin. Somehow they were sure that Karmant would succeed.

"Kevin, due to the recession several companies in India are facing layoffs. Major I.T. companies have also taken a beating. You have probably seen the news of several thousands of people being laid off."

Karmant found Kevin looking down again. It was a sign of disinterest, or disagreement, perhaps. He decided to change focus. After some pause and silence, Kevin looked up again at Karmant.

"You may be wondering what that has to do with this project. Are we sounding like we are making silly excuses, Kevin?"

"Not silly, no. I just can't fathom what recession has got to do with my project."

"Kevin, many people here have family members or partners working in I.T. companies who have lost their jobs. Seeing good companies doing poorly is creating tension here as well. Some of them have taken loans for new homes and cars, and now are watching their finances crumble. So it's been quite a depressing time for them. People are exploring careers outside of I.T. now. While there seems to be recession in the I.T. industry, opportunities in sunrise industries, such as biotech, are booming. There is a lot of uncertainty in the I.T. industry, leading to upheaval and churn. A few good people from your project have left the organization, expecting that layoffs will happen here too. They have either moved out of I.T. or have joined a friend or family member's business to feel more safe. Would you like to know how we are mitigating risks here?"

Kevin nodded affirmatively, with his eyes all on Karmant. Karmant was reassured by Kevin's expression and felt confident that the approach of questioning was helping.

"Last week we called a meeting with all employees to say that we are also concerned about what is happening in the industry, and we assured them of their jobs here. It was then that they were able to get some motivation and gear up for their work again. I'm sure you would know how it feels to see your team living in constant fear. I suggest you address the team as well. Hearing from you would make a big difference. Also, if you give us an extension of twenty-five days we can assure you of the completion of the entire project, along with adequate review."

"Look, I do understand. But twenty-five days is too long a time for us to comply with. What I can give you is an extension of ten days, Karmant."

"Fifteen days. Let's make that final, Kevin. You and your project are very important and a priority to us…"

"No, no! Fifteen days is too much…"

"Look: you address the team and assure them of your trust in us. We will deliver in fifteen days. Anyway, your payment is due only after completion of the project. You will be pleased with the final outcome; I guarantee you this. Please give us this opportunity. I would be happy to walk you through metrics, such as effort variance, where you will see that if not for this wave of resignations, we would have been all set to deliver in advance."

Kevin thought for a while, allowing suspense and a chilling silence to build up.

"Okay… fifteen days is final. Not a day after that. You are indeed good at negotiating, Karmant," Kevin smiled and shook hands with Karmant. "But what if someone else quits?"

"We will announce a project bonus, Kevin," said Mr. Desai. "That will be an added motivation. And it will be on our dime, not yours."

"Jay has already added a couple of backup resources to shadow and learn the work of other team members in case anyone else were to quit. But I believe, with our recent assurance, your address to the team, and Mr. Desai's announcement of a bonus, we should be all set."

"Alright then, show me where the team is. Let's talk to them."

Everyone smiled. They were very content at the outcome of the much-dreaded and important meeting.

Coffee and biscuits were called for. Mr. Desai felt that the coffee was sweeter than before. He was proud of Karmant. Today Karmant was the navigator who sailed the ship to shore.

Karmant added two teaspoons of sugar into his coffee. The meeting room lights were shining on the surface of the coffee like stars. Twinkling stars had come down to him after all.

17

Immediately after the meeting, Mr. Desai took both Jay and Karmant out for lunch to the grand Taj Hotel.

"Karmant, the way you convinced Kevin today was impressive. It was a tough situation, and I was not very optimistic about today's discussion with him, but you turned the tables. Jay… it was good thinking on your part to include Karmant in this meeting."

Jay smiled. "I knew that Karmant would be the best choice to convince Kevin. But even I am surprised about the way he presented the project status to Kevin. His communication was excellent."

Just as they were about to start their lunch, Karmant happened to see Mr. Malhotra. He stood up instantly and greeted him. It was his lucky day today, so he was going to bet on this interaction too.

"Hello, Mr. Malhotra. How are you doing, Sir? It's been a long time since we last spoke," exclaimed Karmant.

"I'm good. Actually I'm in a hurry. I'm here for lunch with my team leaders," Mr. Malhotra replied hesitantly, surprised to see Karmant.

"Oh! That's nice. Why don't you join us until they arrive? We can chat for a while," replied Karmant.

"No, no… actually… I'm not sure if they will be okay with it…"

"Please, for old time's sake. It would be our privilege to get a chance to talk to a knowledgeable person like you."

"No, I'm actually… uhh… What did you say?"

"Sir, I really respected your valuable relationship with our company. I beg you to forgive me for not giving you due respect, and for behaving poorly with you and your managers in the past. It is only due to my bad behavior that our company had to lose a dignified client like you. I am very sorry for whatever has happened."

"Ohh… It's all right. Karmant, you have changed. I am really happy to see you talking in such a graceful way. Fine, let's have lunch together… but I have only thirty minutes. Wait a minute." Mr. Malhotra walked up to his assistant, whispered something in his ear, and returned.

"Okay Karmant, let's join in." Mr. Malhotra joined Karmant, Mr. Desai and Jay, and they had a pleasant meal together. Mr. Malhotra was impressed by the way Karmant talked. He was amazed at the distinguished change in Karmant's communication. Although the conversation was engaging, lunch was a short affair, and then Mr. Malhotra had to leave.

Later, at his desk, Karmant sent Mr. Malhotra a short thank you note. He was surprised to hear back immediately. The email said that Mr. Malhotra would like to give Karmant's organization a second chance and bid for one of their latest projects. Mr. Desai was also copied on the email. No sooner had Karmant finished reading the email than his phone rang. It was an excited Mr. Desai.

Mr. Desai was thrilled, as well as dumbfounded, and asked Karmant to see him in his office.

"Can I come in, Mr. Desai?"

"Yes, Karmant. Please come in," Mr. Desai welcomed Karmant with a delighted smile on his face. However, as soon as Karmant entered the room Mr. Desai's expression turned severe.

"Karmant, you have been a bad example recently because of your communication." Mr. Desai looked at Karmant, and silence between them stretched out.

Karmant took deep breaths and silently muttered to himself, "Now, what is this… Why is he saying 'bad'? I brought him two clients today… Alright… Cool down, Karmant… Just wait before giving any response… Give the right response, Karmant."

Mr. Desai was expecting an immediate reaction from Karmant. When he didn't hear anything from Karmant for some time, he finally broke the silence.

"Karmant, do you want to say anything about what I just told you?"

"Yes, Sir, I truly was a bad communicator in the past," Karmant admitted wholeheartedly.

Mr. Desai's smile returned. "But no longer. I was just teasing you. We have held a review meeting to promote you back into your former position, as well as consider you for the position of vice president of the training department. However, this new position would be confirmed only after monitoring your performance for the next three months. So, how does that sound?"

"I… I don't know… I really don't know what to say Mr. Desai… Oh God… thank you so much GOD…"

"You might want to thank me too."

Both Mr. Desai and Karmant laughed out loud. Mr. Desai was pleased to see the appreciation and delight that Karmant expressed.

Karmant was on top of the world. When he walked out of the office, like always, everyone looked at him with popping eyes.

"Guys, all is well! C'mon, get back to work. Don't stare at me like that. I'm not from a different planet."

Everyone smiled, and Karmant could hear some murmurs of gossip.

He called up Bhavana and asked her to be ready at 7 PM. He was going to take his family out for dinner tonight.

His life was transformed now, and he was full of gratitude to the genie. It was because of the genie that all this had taken place. Overflowing with happiness, he went to spend quality time with special people in his life.

18

Karmant was surprised when Bhavana opened the door. Dressed in an elegant red sari, she looked stunning.

"You look gorgeous, Bhavana! I have never seen you like this before!"

"Thank you. I am still the same old Bhavana, Karmant." Bhavana was nervous and excited. She had been eagerly looking forward to the evening since Karmant's phone call.

"Where is our little one? Raju, look, Papa's home."

Raju came running and held Karmant's legs tight. "Papa! Are we going out somewhere?"

Karmant looked at his little angel. His tiny legs were dressed in full red stretched pants, and he wore a white t-shirt. The red cap that covered his tiny ears rested far down on his forehead and almost touched his eyelashes. Peeping out from his cap, he was the same innocent child who had forgotten all of his papa's anger and was excited to go out. "Children are really God's best creation," Karmant thought.

He had never seen Raju so clearly. With tears in his eyes, he kneeled down beside him to adjust his cap. He looked into his innocent eyes and found the stars twinkling in them. My star he is… my child… he thought. He caught Raju tight in his arms and turned away from Bhavana. Tears trickled from his eyes down to his lips. He had been so unfair to his family… I'm sorry, Raju…

He freshened up and they left for dinner.

He had a joyful dinner, with the love of his life and his baby angel beside him. Raju explored the restaurant, his tiny hands chasing the fish in the aquarium and feet running helter-skelter across the tiles.

Delighted by ice cream and a toy car from the toy shop, Raju felt happier than perhaps he ever had before. On arriving home, Karmant twirled the car into the parking lot. Raju stepped out and leaped to Karmant, signaling that he wanted to be carried.

Karmant took his baby in his arms and playfully got him in his room. Karmant cradled little Raju for some time, and in no time, he had fallen asleep. Karmant looked at him, kissed him on his forehead, and put him to bed.

"I love you, Raju. Papa is very sorry for being angry with you all this while. Thank you for being in my life," he whispered, and left the room.

He stepped into his room and saw Bhavana standing by the window. He gently stood next to her and asked, "Are you alright, Bhavana? Did you enjoy dinner? You didn't talk much tonight."

Bhavana turned to him and started crying. The dam of her silence and patience had broken, and tears flooded from her eyes. She hugged him tight, crying all the while. Karmant understood everything, even though not a word had been uttered. He knew what she had gone through.

With tears rolling down his cheeks, he said in a choked voice, "I am sorry for everything, Bhavana. I've committed offenses against you, and I beg you to forgive me." Both of them hugged each other and cried inconsolably.

After some time, Bhavana looked up and smiled faintly at Karmant. His eyes said it all to her. "Thank you, Bhavana, for being in my life and putting up with me. If it hadn't been for you, I would have lost everything in my life forever. You silently supported me. I needn't even say this, but you are everything I have in my life. You mean the world to me, and I am sorry to have had you go through such turmoil."

Bhavana responded, "All I will say, Karmant, is whatever you are doing every night when you go for a stroll is working."

They both laughed at her comment. Karmant was amazed at how perceptive she was, and was about to tell her about his newfound friend, but Bhavana was too tired to continue their conversation.

Bhavana closed her eyes and thanked God. She was feeling thankful towards everything on Earth. Karmant softly patted her head. Slowly, she fell asleep, the calm and peaceful smile on her face showing her deep contentment and joy at having him back.

Karmant silently moved out of the house. With unhurried steps, he treaded along the path to the beach. He meditated and called out to his best friend.

The genie appeared. "Hello, Karmant. How was your day?"

Karmant calmly replied, "You know, today I understood what silence, patience, and tears mean. I took my family out for dinner today and saw joy and sorrow in their eyes. I lost so much time in being angry at them! My little Raju was so happy today, and so was Bhavana. I feel very sorry for devastating them with my bad communication. If I had continued, I would have lost them forever."

"Cheer up! You have corrected your mistakes in time. Be happy for it, and thank God. It's His timely grace that helped you out," the genie consoled him.

"Indeed, it's His grace that helped me out. Acceptance, forgiveness, and gratitude have helped too. Genie, I am really grateful to you, too. Without your invaluable guidance I wouldn't have come out of my stupor and reached this state. Thank you for being in my life.

I am really thankful to my family too. I have realized the importance of having a family today. We hurt the most whom we love the most."

The genie replied, "Have you ever realized what impact our words have on other people? Whether you express love or anger, or even disinterest, what matters is how it is communicated. Wrong use of words can turn the right feeling into wrong, and make any message into worthless talk or argument. Correct communication and choice of words can make a big difference in building relationships."

Karmant nodded in agreement. "Yes, you're right. The sad thing is that we readily use words to express our hurt, but we seldom realize that it's necessary to express love and give joy through our words."

The genie continued, "Correct communication is the only remedy for healing situations and people, and for building love and trust. Right communication can happen with right thinking. Always think straight, and stay true to yourself as well as others. If this principle is followed, our communication will be free from deceit and misunderstandings. It must always be understood and consciously remembered that right communication builds mutual love and trust, and is the foundation for harmonious relationships.

Let me also ask you this: Do you sleep well? Or do you feel deprived of sleep even if you sleep for a long duration? Do you tend to be preoccupied with too many concerns? Are you plagued with too many dreams?"

"Yes, Genie," replied Karmant.

"That is the result of incomplete communication. Sometimes people become angry over small petty issues and stop talking to others for hours, or even days. It is necessary that we have complete communication with everyone.

I will tell you a story to explain it better. There was a man who diligently looked after his family and performed his duties towards them. He took great pains to keep them happy. One day his close friend commented,

'You are a real gem of a person. You sacrificed your dreams for the sake of your family. You've given them your entire life and all of your time for so many years. You ensured that their dreams were fulfilled. You are really a great human being.'

Listening to this, the man's eyes welled up with tears, and he silently started crying. His friend anxiously asked, 'What happened? I was appreciating you for all that you've done. What made you cry?' The man, still with tears in his eyes, replied, 'I've been waiting to hear that all my life. I wanted someone to notice and appreciate me for all that I have done all my life for my family. You are the first person who has acknowledged me. I feel so good today, to see that someone values my sacrifices,' and saying this he began sobbing again.

Appreciating someone for what they do is also an important facet of communication," the genie explained.

Karmant drank in this information. "Genie, could you give me some examples of wrong communication, and the correct substitute for each example?"

"Okay." The genie twirled his fingers and made words appear on the sand.

"Here, read this."

Wrong communication: You are really stupid, and you can't ever do anything right.

Right communication: You have done well, but you can still improve further with some more effort.

Wrong communication: You always want to be with your friends. You don't love me.

Right communication: I don't mind you spending time with your friends, but I would like it if you spend some more time with me.

Wrong communication: You are so selfish; you always think only of yourself.

Right communication: Please don't behave like this. I feel bad when you behave like this. We can find a better way together.

Wrong communication: You are always late.

Right communication: I feel bad when you don't show up at time you have promised.

Karmant nodded. "These are great, Genie."

"And here are few more examples of right and wrong communication with yourself."

"Do you mean self-talk?"

"Yes. Read on. These are self-explanatory."

Wrong communication: I will never be able to buy this car, as it is very expensive.

Right communication: I will not be able to buy this car now. But if I want, I can earn enough money to buy it.

Wrong communication: Problems always come to me. There will never be a day that goes well for me.

Right communication: Problems come to everyone; I am no exception. I will face each problem courageously.

Wrong communication: I can never get anything right.

Right communication: What should I do to rectify this situation? I can learn from mistakes and make progress everytime.

"And remember, Karmant," the genie continued, "Even more important than the right choice of words are the right feelings. Libraries and bookshops are filled with books on what to say and what not to say, but many of them fail to tell you to clear your slate. If a slate is already filled with writing, even if you write the right words, they will be indecipherable and ineffective. Generate the right feelings through the practices of forgiveness, acceptance and gratitude, and the right words will follow."

19

"Genie, I am glad that I have begun to learn ways to master the tough art of communication."

The genie exclaimed, "Tough art? Communication is the most natural and spontaneous thing to do. In fact, there is nothing tough about it. That's just a myth, a wrong belief that many have."

"If communication is so natural and spontaneous, then why does it seem so difficult?"

"Every child is a natural communicator. A tiny baby can communicate hunger, and even anger, without words. There is integrity between his feelings, thoughts, speech, and action. Later, as the child learns to speak, it's a joy to hear him speak from the heart and communicate innocently. With time, the child learns to add artifice to his communication and feelings, and thus makes the simplest thing in the world complicated."

"I can relate to that. As a small child, Raju used to rush towards me and hold me tight whenever I was back from work. But as time passed, his behavior changed. Of late, he assesses my mood and then decides his response accordingly. If I raise my voice, he just runs away from me. Today he held me tight when he saw that I was happy."

"Children are very good at sensing your feelings. And like children, every adult has the ability to sense others' feelings, but many have chosen to ignore it. They focus just on conveying their message and not on sensing how the other person is feeling. There are other aspects of non-verbal communication which people rarely pay heed to."

"I always thought that my words communicated what I wanted to. I've never focused on non-verbal communication, even though I have read that it is important."

"A message hasn't been communicated successfully unless the receiver understands it completely. Context is the way a message is delivered, and it is also known as paralanguage. Most adults focus only on language. But paralanguage includes non-verbal elements in speech such as the tone of voice, body language, expression in the sender's eyes, hand gestures, and the state of emotions. All this is to do with the person communicating. At the same time, the speaker has to sense the feelings of the listener too."

"I have read in the past that communication is 7% words, 35% voice and 55% body language. But again, I find it difficult to believe."

"Wait a minute, Karmant. The percentages you just rattled off are also a myth. Sometimes a fancy idea is repeated often enough that everyone believes it. Those percentages come from a complete misrepresentation of research conducted in the 1960s. They were from a very small and uniform sample of volunteers who were tested with just single words with only the face visible. The Professor who conducted the research has himself gone on record several times to say that it is difficult to extract any meaningful figure from the percentages that came up in this one single experiment. That said, it is true that non-verbal communication plays a big role in communication."

"So, Genie, how does one learn to focus on so many aspects of non-verbal communication? Just goes to prove my point that mastering communication is difficult," said Karmant with a wink.

"Haha, Karmant. Your wink says it all. I think just keeping one thing in mind is enough to take care of all non-verbal communication: be congruent."

"Congruent as in…?" Karmant interrupted.

"Congruency in words, thoughts, actions, and feelings. Sometimes a person's emotions convey a different meaning than what he speaks, and his actions are not at all congruent with his words. As humans, we believe what we see more than what we hear, and we trust the accuracy of the non-verbal behavior more than the verbal behavior. So when we communicate, the other person consciously and subconsciously notices any mismatch between words, thoughts, feelings and action," the genie explained.

"Hmmm. That is indeed simple. All I have to do is be truthful to my feelings and constantly make sure my thoughts, words, feelings, and actions are in alignment"

"Just notice if they are not congruent, and they will become congruent the moment you notice."

"Wow. Just noticing. I am eager to give that a try. Thank you for this wonderful tip, Genie."

"Now, Karmant, let us get some practice. Try thanking me without meaning it."

Karmant tried to blurt out thanks without meaning it, but he stammered and frowned at his own words.

"Seems very funny, Genie."

"Yes, it feels funny, because you are now aware. In the daily hustle and bustle of life, we forget to notice. If you begin noticing, you will find something strange when your communication is not in alignment, and it will automatically realign. It is indeed simple, Karmant. Hopefully you will no longer hold on to the belief that communication is difficult."

"No, Genie. With all I've experienced in just few days of meeting you, and with the clarity you provided today, I no longer believe that. Is there anything else you can tell me today?"

"Yes, I can tell you some of the many myths about communication: 'I have a poor personality, therefore I am not a good communicator,' 'I must feel confident before I can communicate well,' 'Only those who have language fluency can communicate well.' As you can see, all these beliefs stem from the fact that we have made communication—a very natural and easy thing—this big difficult monster to be tackled.

"What about the conflict management aspect of communication, Genie? That is something that definitely requires attention. I have read about styles of conflict management, and about levels of teaming behaviors. I do believe conflict management is not an easy thing. Am I mistaken about that too?"

The genie gently reminded Karmant, "We have already seen different types of responses: quick response, rash or aggressive response, patient and analytical response, placative or passive response, and complete response. We have already discussed different styles of managing conflicts. We have also seen different ways of managing conflict: diffuse anger, put yourself into others' shoes, take responsibility for your feelings, show respect. If you stick to a fixed, default response, it leads to conflict. If you are flexible in your responses, you make yourself amenable in a given situation. You can then peacefully and mutually agree upon a solution with others, and the conflict will disappear. Many times, heart to heart communication resolves conflicts better than lengthy brainstorming discussions."

"That's splendid. So, the solution lies in complete response. Yes, I understood now. I also understood the ways of managing conflicts. Thank you for all this information. I will examine what other beliefs I have, and also immediately put into practice bringing congruency in my communication. Er, I mean, noticing if I am congruent or not…"

"Ha ha! I am happy that you are sincerely working on the takeaways from our daily conversations," the genie laughed heartily.

20

"Genie, there is something else bothering me: my relationship with my son. How can I be a better parent?"

"Good parenting is all about right communication. Tell me, how do you communicate with Raju?"

"Of late I've been busy with my work, and my communication with Raju has been very minimal. In the morning, when I get ready to go to work, he goes to his preschool. When I return from work at night, many times he is busy finishing his homework with Bhavana or is off to sleep. In retrospect, I can see that most times I shout at him. I blow my top when I see his toys, school bag, and shoes being strewn around."

"When was the last time you shouted at him?"

"Last week, when he broke a flower pot, I shouted at him, 'Why did you break it? When will you grow up? Why don't you listen?'"

"What did he answer then?"

"For some time he was quiet and didn't answer. I couldn't control my anger and started shouting him even more, prodding him to give me the reason. He was frightened and told me that the flower pot was already on the edge of the table, that it wasn't his mistake. Then I warned him to be more careful next time."

"Karmant, that's exactly what many parents do. Such interrogation forces children to lie and make up stories in order to escape punishment. It's very easy for them to develop the tendency to lie and blame others. This tendency or pattern of blaming others is called the 'blamer pattern', which gets deep-rooted into their nature."

"Yes, I see. I didn't realize the consequences of my behavior at that time. How should I communicate with him at times like that?"

"Communication with children does not just mean talking to them; it also means exchange of thoughts, appreciating them at the right time, giving them appropriate punishment, or even forgiving them for the mistakes they make. Forgiving them doesn't mean forgetting the mistakes, but making them aware of the consequences of their actions and giving them suggestions and guidance so that they do not repeat the same mistakes. Children have the right to make mistakes, but we should not focus on their mistakes.

In this case, instead of rebuking Raju, you could have asked him, 'What did you learn from this incident?' When parents point out children's mistakes in correct words, children learn from their mistakes. Using right words with your child has a great impact on his development and well-being."

"Genie, you are all-knowing. You're right, that is exactly what happens with me. When I get angry I keep rebuking him, 'Yesterday you broke a glass. Today you broke the flower pot. What are you going to break tomorrow?' Sometimes, when we have guests at home, I even tell them, 'Our son is very mischievous. He has broken several windows in the neighborhood.'"

The genie nodded gravely. "And so, many times parents present a wrong image of their own children. Where is your focus when you speak about your child? The more you concentrate on their mistakes, the more mistakes they will make. Also, when they do something good, do you pay attention to it? When your child gets good grades on a test, do you say, 'My child is so clever! He studied really hard and earned this good grade! If he studies better, he will be at the top of the class?'

If he has won a race, appreciate and encourage him by saying, 'What a swift sprinter you are! One day you will certainly become a good athlete.'"

Karmant's expression grew grim and contemplative. "I realize that I never appreciate him. Poor Raju tries to show me his paintings, but I don't pay any mind. The next time when he shows me his paintings, I will appreciate and encourage him."

"That's good, Karmant! Positive words empower us with health and enthusiasm. So, always use inspirational and optimistic words with your children."

"Could you give me some examples?"

"If a child is shouting and his father shouts back at him to make him quiet, the child thinks, 'If I am wrong for shouting, then what's my father doing? He is shouting at me too.' If he calmly says, 'Speak softly', instead of shouting a command not to shout, then the child will listen to him.

The use of positive words will steer your child away from negative words. If you want your child to be more confident and successful, use positive words to build his confidence instead of threatening or scaring him. Every child has the right to express negative feelings. For example, if a child is crying for something and you shout at him to make him quiet, he will become quiet. But this will develop a 'blaster' pattern: he will suppress anger within, and one day it will blast out destructively; he may scream terrible words or start breaking things. Instead of shouting at him, ask, 'What do you want? What has happened?' This will help him to open up and freely express his feelings."

"Now I understand why Raju suddenly stops crying as soon as he sees me. If he insists on something, Bhavana threatens him that she will complain to me. I really need to help him open up."

"You're right, Karmant. Give him enough time to express himself, understand what he is trying to communicate, and then act accordingly. If we desire cooperation from our children, we need to carefully consider the way we communicate with them: our tone, choice of words, feelings, intention, and body language. Children generally cooperate when we talk to them in the right manner.

For example, a father says to his child, 'Get a glass of water for me.' What tone did he use? Does it sound more like words full of love or an order? When speaking with love, the father shows the child appreciation by saying, 'Good boy' when he brings the water. The child is also happy. Then imagine, after some time the child breaks a tea cup while playing, and the father shouts at him, 'You are an idiot… Good for nothing!'

The child is confused. He wonders, 'Just a while ago I was a good boy, so now how did I become bad?' The child is too young. He does not understand how two things so different could be said to him. He has simply made a mistake. So what? Did he do it deliberately? No. But the parents believe it was done deliberately, and express that accusation through their words. They choose wrong words, which become wrong communication, which in turn slows down the emotional growth of the child tremendously."

"I never realized my careless words would affect him so badly. How can I do better?"

The genie continued, "If a child fails his exams, never tell him, 'You have failed.' Instead say, 'You have not been successful yet.' These words will help the child overcome his depression.

So the secret of complete parenting is simple: improve your communication with your child and make yourself available to him through positive communication. Understand how your child learns. Having meaningful conversation with your child is the key to conscious parenting. Come, let's practice. I will tell you some statements that parents usually tell children, and you can tell me what a better response could be in light of what we have talked about today."

"Yes, Genie, please go on."

"Take this first one: Stop shouting and getting angry. Your temper tantrums are not going to work with me."

"I think better response could be: You don't need to get angry. You can get what you want without getting angry."

"Well done, Karmant! How about this one: You are a failure. You can't do anything right. Idiot!"

"Even though you haven't been successful this time, our love for you will never diminish."

"Superb! Take the next one: You are wrong."

"I think it could be: You've made a mistake, but you can easily correct it."

"Wonderful! Now, tell me this one. A child asks his father, 'Daddy, shall I do this?' The father answers, 'No.'"

"Probably the father could answer, 'Certainly. But, consider this alternative…'"

"Good! And the next one: Don't bang the door."

"That's easy. 'Close the door smoothly.'"

"Now, this is the last one: Keep quiet. Shut up."

"The parents could probably ask the child, 'What do you want?' Or if they are getting too disturbed, then they could tell the child, 'I want to be myself in silence for a while.'"

"Karmant, that was nice participation from your side! I hope this gave you clarity on correct parenting. If parents want their children to fulfill their expectations, then they must reflect: do they give their children all that they need? Are they creating the right environment for their child to grow and blossom, to fulfill the dreams that they have seen for him? If you want your child to imbibe the qualities of Jesus, you have to imbibe the qualities of Mother Mary."

Karmant's heart was overflowing with gratitude. In a choked voice, he said, "This was really an important lesson for me. I will be a good parent to my little Raju. I will never treat him badly or say rude words to him. Thank you, Genie, for all the guidance."

"You are welcome. Have a nice day tomorrow, and do well in the review."

"Hey, Genie... how did you know I have a review tomorrow?"

The genie laughed aloud and said, "My friend, you are forgetting... I am a genie."

"Oh. Yes! Do you have a specific word of advice for my meeting tomorrow?"

"Keep this mantra in mind: Don't impress, just express." With that, the genie disappeared into the mysterious realm of his existence.

Karmant walked the path back to his home. He looked up at the stars. It had been a twinkling sort of day for him. He called up to the stars, "Can you hear me? Oh... I know you can't. But I want to tell you today that you are special to me, and so is your twinkle. You have filled my day with brightness. Thank you."

Karmant was still lovingly smiling at the stars as he drifted off to sleep. He had seen twinkling in so many ways today... in a coffee cup... in Raju's eyes... in Bhavana's tears. He fell asleep with his heart full of one thought: "Thank you, Genie..."

21

The boardroom was hot and humid, as the air conditioner had just broken down. It was Karmant's review meeting. He was seated at the far end of the table, diagonally opposite Mr. Desai, amidst all the board members and Jay. Everyone was waiting for the chairman.

From the corner of his eye, Karmant noticed everyone's eyes were glued to him. After all, it was his D-day. The news of his review had spread like wildfire. Everyone was curious to know the outcome.

In that pin-drop silence, Karmant sensed the stress in the environment. He assured himself, "Relax Karmant," and started observing his breath. His breath was shallow and rapid. His mouth was dry. He took two deep breaths and gulped a glass of water. He was now feeling much fresher.

The chairman arrived and sat at the head of the table. He quickly glanced at Karmant and began. "Karmant, your latest interactions with clients and colleagues have been exemplary. Thanks to your efforts, we have been able to retain a client that we were on the verge of losing. The board has unanimously agreed on restoring you to your old position. What do you have to say about this?"

"I sincerely thank Jay and Mr. Desai for trusting me and allowing me to participate in the meeting with Kevin. I am happy with this remarkable turnaround in my career."

Other board members went at him, one after the other.

"Do you think you can justify the promotion, if you get it?"

"Yes, Sir!"

"Do you think you can do justice to the work and the position, and do you realize that when you are in that position the company's image rests on your shoulders?"

"Yes, Sir, I do."

"You have had a history of aggressive behavior, and have behaved rudely with your clients and subordinates in the past. What do you have to say to that?"

"I am sorry for what I did. I had the opportunity recently to reflect on my behavior and have learnt my lessons. Getting work done was never a problem for me, but I have learned the hard way that 'how to get it done' is more important," said Karmant, with tension building up in his nerves.

"Why do you now feel that you can perform better and change what went wrong? It's true, you have proved it to some extent with the recent successful meetings you had with clients. But this is my concern: this motivation needs to last. So, why do you feel you are ready to return?"

"Sir, I have changed a lot. I have turned to a mentor outside the organization who has helped me learn a lot about communication and collaboration. Even while at the meeting with Kevin, it was I who…" He abruptly stopped, and the advice, 'Don't impress, just express,' flashed through his mind, changing his perspective.

"…I mean, all I had to do was ask the right questions. Ultimately, me, Mr. Desai and Jay came through as a team. I realize that in the past I made many mistakes and did not have the right attitude. I never understood the meaning of the terms 'patience' and 'collaboration'. Now I feel I have become sensitive towards the subtler aspects of human relationships, and am able to empathize with others. The demotion has helped me in a big way. And the best part is that I am determined to stick to the new lessons that I have learned into the future, serving this company."

Everyone was impressed, pleased by his humility and the sincere feelings in his words.

"Very well, Karmant. We'll give you a chance, and would like to restore your former designation. Also, as Mr. Desai would have mentioned, after evaluating your performance for the next three months we will decide if you can take up the additional responsibilities of the training department. We would like to see all our employees benefit from your example and become better people at work."

"Thank you very much, Sir! Thank you, gentlemen! I am really grateful to all of you for this opportunity. There is just one thing that I would like to ask, Sir, with Mr. Desai's and your permission."

"Yes. Please go ahead."

"Due to the demotion I have been through a lot of stress, and so has my family. I have a little Raju… ah… a little boy. I haven't spent any quality time with him or with my wife. With your permission, I wish to take a holiday with them, for a week. Of course, that is, if there is no important work at the office, or any…"

Mr. Desai interrupted, "Please go ahead. I think we can take care of the work for a week's time."

The chairman concurred, "Very well, please follow Mr. Desai's suggestion and enjoy your well-deserved vacation. Okay gentlemen, let's end the review meeting here and congratulate Mr. Karmant for his efforts. We wish you all the best." The chairman concluded the review meeting on a good note.

Everyone congratulated Karmant and wished him a good vacation. He was all smiles. He quickly rushed to the company help desk to arrange for his family vacation.

He rushed back home excitedly and announced the vacation to Bhavana. Bhavana was thrilled. Little Raju, enthusiastic as ever, hopped around joyously when he heard about the holiday.

22

Everything was falling in place. The demotion had proved to be a blessing: it had given him back the spirit of his life.

"What next steps will the genie lead me to?" Karmant thought as he headed towards the beach. The genie arrived shortly after Karmant had completed his meditation.

"Are you ready to take on the world now?" asked the genie.

"Yes, Genie! I'm really happy with the way things have turned out and would like to thank you for bringing about this change in me. In fact, you have completely transformed me. You helped me to cross the most difficult path of my life. I will cherish your lessons, I will practice and preach them all my life. Thank you so much!" Karmant exclaimed.

"Karmant, as a genie I am meant to touch people's lives in different ways. I am glad you took your lessons seriously. Now, tell me: if you were given a chance to work for God, would you take it?"

"Yes! Of course... Who would not take it?"

"Okay, I can show you how to work for God. We will now discuss how to work unconditionally and impersonally, and how to have supreme and divine communication with God."

Karmant was desperate to hear something like this. He had never imagined that he would ever be introduced to such knowledge. "Please, tell me quickly… I am eager to know."

"First, tell me, what's the purpose of your life: your personal ambition as well as your collective ambition?"

Karmant quickly replied, "I am working as a senior operations manager and aspire to be the CEO of the company soon."

"This is your personal ambition. Okay! Now, let's divide it into three parts: 'I am' is Part 1, 'it is' is Part 2, and 'so that' is Part 3.

The answer to Part 1 is who you want to be, or your role. It is better to phrase it as 'I am' instead of 'I will,' so that your mind will bring forth the vision into your life. The answer to Part 2 should comprise what you will do and how you will do it. The answer to Part 3 is the impact you will have on others, and on humanity as a whole. It should describe an impersonal goal. Personal ambitions lead to struggle, but impersonal ambitions lead towards peace."

"Could you explain that again, with an example?"

"Sure! The personal and collective ambition for a carpenter could be: I am an expert carpenter who builds comfortable furniture so that people can experience higher levels of consciousness comfortably.

Now, tell me, which of the three parts is most important to you?" the genie asked, carefully watching Karmant's expressions.

"According to what I have understood so far, Part 1 and Part 2 seem to be important to me."

"If it is Part 1, then you have clear vision. If Part 2, then you have clarity about how to accomplish your mission. If Part 3 seems most important, then you have an impersonal vision as well as an impersonal mission. It's good that you have moved a bit beyond keeping part 1 as your only goal. Many people stop at Part 1. They say, 'I will be a doctor' … that's it. Some people aspire to more and say they will be the best doctor. But a true leader is one who is clear about the impact his role shall have on humanity."

"So I can word my ambition as: I am a CEO who runs one of the largest I.T. companies successfully, so that the world can experience innovation and progress further through technological advancement."

"Yes, that's very right. Keep in mind that whatever you keep your focus on, that is what you will become. If your focus is on Part 1, 'I am,' you may end up just being a CEO. By merely playing a role you will have achieved your personal vision. If your focus is on Part 2, 'who is,' you may end up playing a key function at a large I.T. multinational. You may or may not be its CEO. You would achieve your mission of running one of the largest I.T. multinationals successfully, which is better than just aspiring to be a CEO. That is focusing on both a personal vision and a mission; who you shall be and how you shall do it.

But the key focus must be on Part 3. All great leaders focus on Part 3. If your focus is on Part 3, 'so that,' then you are cultivating an impersonal vision. If your focus is on how the world can experience innovation and be better off through technological advancement, you will leave no stone unturned to bring about a mass transformation in the world through technological advancement. If that is truly your focus, it will not matter to you whether you are a CEO or helping to run a large multinational successfully. All that will matter to you is whether you are causing innovation in I.T. and making the world a better place. Titles and methods become a means to achieve an end."

"So, you mean to say that if my focus is on Part 3, I have an impersonal goal."

"Yes, you've got it right."

"But why does it matter whether my goal is personal or impersonal?"

"Simply focusing on an impersonal goal will change your outlook towards your work. You will have new insight into everything that you will undertake, and supreme ambition. It will be an experience like you have never tasted before in your life."

"How is that possible?"

"Let's understand it with a story…

There was once a king who wanted to abandon all his responsibilities and his kingdom so that he could devote more time to his spiritual quest. He pondered for a long time, and finally decided to seek guidance from his spiritual master. He explained, 'O Master, I am unable to get any suitable heir to the throne. My son is too young to handle the duties of the kingdom. The day I get a suitable heir, I will relinquish all my responsibilities to him and spend the rest of my life in search of God.'

The master quipped, 'Do you find anyone worthier than me?'

The king was overjoyed. 'Who else can understand my kingdom better than you? From this moment onwards, I surrender my kingdom to you.'

The master then asked, 'What will you do now?'

The king replied, 'I will set aside a small portion from the treasury to meet my basic needs for the rest of my life.'

'But the treasures are all mine now. I will not let you take anything from it,' answered the master.

The king remorsefully said, 'Okay… I will earn my livelihood by working somewhere.'

'Well, if you have decided to work, then I have a vacancy. Would you want to take it up?' the master enquired with a half-smile on his lips.

The king grasped the opportunity and said, 'Yes… I am ready to take it up.'

The master looked at him and said, 'I have a vacancy for the post of a king. I want you to work as a king and take your salary every month from the treasury.' The king agreed to it.

After a year, when the master returned, he found that the king was relaxed and at peace. He had found a way to devote time to his spiritual quest while performing his job as a ruler.

So, what changed? Nothing at all! The same kingdom, the same king, the same job of ruling! All that had changed was his perspective."

"What a wonderful story! Now I completely understand the point, Genie."

"I had asked you whether you would like to work for God. In order to do so, you must keep an impersonal outlook. Mahatma Gandhi aspired for the freedom of India, without being bothered over who would become the prime minister or the president of a free India. That is why he is considered a great leader. This is what differentiates leaders from great leaders: leaders have a vision, but great leaders have an impersonal vision. Swami Vivekananda's vision was that of universal Vedanta. His focus and vision were not limited to being the chief of the Ramakrishna Mission, or to simply grow and multiply the foundation's activities."

"Indeed, even I consider them to be great leaders. So, this is the underlying reason behind their greatness."

"They kept an impersonal goal. Their focus on Part 3 helped them achieve this greatness. They were working for God."

"Genie, how can I start acting on an impersonal vision? What task should I undertake? And will I be able to complete it?"

"Nature especially helps those with the highest goals. When you decide to help humanity and take up an impersonal intention, nature, with all its forces, will come to your aid. Once you decide your goal, take small steps to imbibe all those virtues which will help you to achieve your goals.

Start with small steps. While working in your organization, if you are not clear about your impersonal goal, set a smaller goal without thinking about whether it's aligning in the right direction. Take up a social activity. You can work at an NGO, or even serve at an orphanage, after your work hours as per your convenience. When you climb the mountain and reach the pinnacle of service, you will get your direction. You may even realize that the NGO or the orphanage where you are serving regularly is not really encouraging you; what inspires you is spending time with children and teaching them to be independent. When this becomes clear, you can take the initiative to teach children. Now you have reached the second mountain. Going forward, you may even see another goal which will fill you with so much ecstasy and energy that everything else will look and feel smaller in comparison to it.

And so, if you're unclear about your goal, working towards any goal will put you on the right path to finding your right goal, and the purpose and ambition of your life. You may have to climb two or three mountains, but finally you will reach the pinnacle."

"But I don't have spare time after office hours to get engaged in any such activity. Does this mean I won't be able to live an impersonal life?"

"No, my friend! You can keep an impersonal intention while performing your present job. Even if what you do may seem personal, when you combine it with an impersonal intention, it can change to an impersonal goal.

As an example, let's understand how a television sets' dealer can work with an impersonal intention. He can have the frame of mind that he is not just selling idiot boxes, but a medium which will use entertainment to bring joy and knowledge to every member of the family. He could glue some stickers creatively on the television sets which would caution the families that they must not get too attached to the programs shown on television. He could also distribute printouts with a schedule of some good programs."

"Wow! You have such wonderful ideas, Genie. Could you change to a human form and join my company? I can create a powerful position for you," Karmant proposed, and both broke into laughter.

"Thank you, but I am very satisfied in this work that I do for God."

"I work in the corporate sector. Please tell me, how can I keep an impersonal vision?"

"Actually, many corporations do not keep an impersonal vision. Some of them keep an impersonal goal, but don't take it seriously. Some of them state a goal, but don't fit it into their work structure.

Leadership lessons and surveys point to the principle that a group must always aim for a motivated and uplifting vision. Such a vision does not necessarily come down from the people high in the hierarchy. Every corporate team, however small or however ranked in the corporate ladder, can link the company's vision to an impersonal vision."

"Really!? Can this really be done?"

"Yes! Let's assume your corporate team needs to deliver a software project in a span of three months. If the team wishes to get motivated to complete it on time, it must ask itself, 'What change will this software project bring about in the world? What will be its impact on humanity at large?' If they become aware that their project will help thousands of employees as well as their customers, as it will help boost the productivity of their employees, then they will broaden their personal vision to an impersonal vision. Then, boosting the productivity of employees may become the main goal, irrespective of whether the project succeeds or fails. Your team may add other features to the project which you would have never thought of before.

You can even write a research paper or blog on the steps involved in the making of your project, which can benefit other people. You can write or share your thoughts with others for free. When corporate teams link their corporate goals with an impersonal vision, they offer themselves to a higher goal.

Say there is another team that has to prepare a financial report in a month's time. While working on the project, they can set the impersonal goal of mastering the principles of finances and learning every minute financial detail, to help build an efficient and strong knowledge base for the company. This knowledge base may be used for training purposes.

Let's understand this better with one more example. Why is it that when any country is struggling for freedom, all people unite and fight together, but when the struggle comes to an end, they start fighting with each other? They all had a unique, common, and higher objective to achieve until they attained freedom. Likewise, corporate teams must aim towards a higher, common objective. Even though very few corporate teams tread this path, they must think in such ways. Instead of merely functioning as a team, they should strengthen and awaken their presence in such a way that those who watch them will be inspired to follow in their footsteps."

Karmant frowned, thinking over all he had heard. "Now, I understand that if we attach an impersonal vision to whatever we do, we will work for God. But does the profession matter in any way? For example, if a person selling liquor attaches an impersonal goal to his work, can we call it an impersonal service for God?"

"Karmant, you must not attach an impersonal goal only for its namesake. Liquor doesn't help to raise the level of consciousness in any way; instead it acts to lower it. You must select a profession in which the expression of the impersonal goal becomes easy.

While performing your job, honestly ask yourself, 'How can I make my work impersonal? Am I really working for God?' Do not have narrow minded, limited thinking, like 'All profit should come to me,' or, 'this work should only be done in this particular way.' Every work has a creative edge to it that can be explored."

"Genie, I'm feeling motivated now to work along these lines. I promise to attach an impersonal vision to all work that I undertake. Just thinking about it is inspiring! I am grateful to you for these lessons. You have taught me something unique today, something I never knew."

"Don't thank me; thank God."

"Is there even a way to thank God? What you've told me so far is amazing, but this is for the first time I've heard of this point. I can't grasp it. Could you please elaborate?"

"It's very simple to understand. Let's assume that you want to thank someone who has helped you in a big way. You decide to visit him. When you reach his home, you are shocked at what you see. He is writing something, seated at a table. Suddenly there's a gush of wind, and the pages are strewn around. With one hand he tries to hold the papers to prevent them from flying away, and with the other hand he tries to shut the window. You see him struggle. Then suddenly there is a power failure, and he is in search of candles. What will you do? Will you say, 'I had come to thank you, so I'll just thank you and leave now?'"

"Oh no! I will help him first!"

"Correct. Even though you had gone to thank him, helping him will automatically come to you. On your own you will want to pick up his papers, to close the window and light the candle for him. He may be managing it all and not troubled by it, but that does not mean that you should not help."

"What are you trying to say, Genie?" Karmant asked, with confusion and a bit of impatience.

"Karmant, think about it. How would you thank God? You would offer him help out of the sense of gratitude that rises within you. You would at least help him find a matchstick for the candle, hold the candle and help him light it. Thus, you must thank God not just with words, but with action. With every impersonal action, you are helping God. That is the way to thank Him in the truest sense."

Karmant nodded, with an expression of excitement and resolve.

"By the way, my dear friend, I had given you a hint about this on the first day. Do you remember it?" asked the genie, with teasing in his voice.

"On the first day? I don't remember!"

"I had mentioned that there were four ways to solve your problem, and you chose the third way; it appealed the most to you. I had even mentioned to you that the fourth way is an extension of 'Changing your outlook.'"

"Oh yes! I remember it a little. But that point was not very clear to me then."

"Now you know that changing your outlook towards your job means looking at it from an impersonal point of view. As you do so, you start developing interest in it."

"Oh, yes! Now I understood. You have explained to me the true purpose of living life, and the way to find bliss. I will work on this fourth way."

"Do you know that God can help you in this task?"

"Really! How?"

"You just have to ask God for help. Communicate with Him."

"Communicate with God? That's amazing!"

"I will tell you about it tomorrow." The genie signaled his time for departure.

"Okay friend. See you tomorrow."

As he walked home, Karmant was full of thoughts. This new talk had filled him with immense energy, a drive to work for an impersonal goal, and the desire to work for God. What could be better? Having the supreme desire, free of ego and selfish motives, brimming with impersonal ideas, free from any material competition.

A feeling of gratitude towards the genie emerged in him. Without the genie, he thought, I would not have understood any of this, impersonal vision and working for God in turn. Now, as I understand it, it is my duty to share it with others. The genie has changed my life…

Karmant drifted off to sleep, full of thankfulness.

23

Early the next morning Karmant woke up to his dreams. He had been dreaming about work and his team. He joined his hands together and prayed, "Dear God, thank you very much. I want to help you, not just with my words, but with my deeds. Please help me in doing this."

It being a Sunday, Bhavana was surprised to see Karmant awake so early. She gently asked, "Today is a Sunday. You can sleep for longer if you wish. I'll get you tea in some time."

"No, Bhavana, it's okay. Even though it's a Sunday, I have some work to complete today," replied Karmant, with fresh eyes and a glowing smile on his face.

"Okay, I'll get you some tea." Bhavana noticed an excitement in Karmant's eyes, instead of the usual burdened feeling.

Throughout the day, Karmant was busy writing something in his study. When Bhavana saw him leaving his study in the evening, he was still as fresh and lively as he was in the morning. She wondered what kept him so fresh in spite of a long day of work.

Soon another night of lessons arrived, and Karmant stepped out onto the sand. With every step forward, his thoughts skipped steps forward too.

He meditated deeply. The sheer wonder of witnessing life events as mere thoughts that rise and fall was a revelation for Karmant. The practice of meditation had brought him this eye of wisdom, where those very events that used to trouble him earlier no longer touched him. He could watch them in a detached manner, marveling at the possibility of freedom and joy that this brought him.

"Hello friend, how are you?" asked the genie, with his perpetual astounding smile.

"I have felt so fresh today, Genie. The new purpose to my life has filled me with enthusiasm, excitement and joy."

"That's very good news. So, what's the purpose you have written?"

"I am an innovator in the field of human excellence who helps others release their potential exponentially, so that the level of happiness and productivity in the world multiplies."

"That's nice! Which part of the sentence is most important to you?"

"I am now clear that it is Part 3: I want to impact the productivity and happiness of the world. Just thinking about it fills me with energy."

"I notice that you have changed the CEO part to innovator," said the genie with a mischievous smile. "This feeling of energy you have—that is what working for God is all about."

"I can see how this feels like working for a divine purpose—a higher purpose."

"Okay. Now that you are working for God, do you know how to communicate with God?"

"Do you mean, how do I pray?"

"No. I mean, as you feel energized by a higher purpose, do you know how to receive higher messages, deeper hints about life and its higher purpose? I call this as communication with God."

"Sort of divine communication?" asked Karmant curiously.

"More of letting the divine communicate with you. It is about connecting to God, to a divine power, and receiving what is being said to you."

"Genie, how do I recognize that God is connecting with me and talking to me?"

"By knowing that you are either Ms. Eyes or Mr. Ears or Dr. Feelings!"

"What? What is this? Who are all these people?"

"Before we proceed, always remember this lesson: never get stuck on words. Words are just a medium to express feelings. Be it an expression of love or faith, or anything else, the feeling behind the words is more important. Words are like the stick that holds an ice cream bar. As you consume the ice cream the stick's purpose is served, and it is thrown away. Similarly, once words convey the meaning or feeling behind them, you must not pay attention to the words that are used. They are just a medium."

"Okay, I got it. So, who are the people you just mentioned? What is their meaning, if any?"

"Just as words are a medium, so too are these names. I am using them to make things simple and help you understand better. They are independent of any gender. Some people are Ms. Eyes, who receive guidance from God through visuals. Such people's memory is also visual and they can't grasp words as easily as pictures. They decode those pictures and work accordingly. Some people are Mr. Ears, who receive guidance through listening to the voice within them. Such people are more attuned to spoken words. And lastly, Dr. Feelings are those who receive guidance through a certain feeling or vibration in their body. They don't catch words, nor do they see any pictures. They decode their message with the help of what they feel. The prefix Dr. has been added because they can easily grasp others' vibes or feelings, and distinguish between the positive and the negative based on that. They believe in something which they do not see or hear; that is why they often believe in the unseen or unheard.

These are three different types of people. As per the body-mind mechanism of a person, he may excel at one thing while the other gets awakened within him. He may be most receptive towards the voice he hears, but he may also be able to grasp feelings at times: this means Mr. Ears is predominant in him and Dr. Feelings is gradually gaining strength. First, you must know which category you belong to. God sends his messages in several forms, and people receive them through what they feel is the most comfortable and simplest medium for them. When you are aware of the way you receive God's messages, God then reciprocates to you in that form. Do you understand this, Karmant?"

"Yes. It's a beautiful thing that I already practice, but I was not aware of what it meant. I understand this well. My wife, Bhavana, has the nature of Dr. Feelings. Before she listens to something she already senses if it is good or bad. Once we went to see a beautiful bungalow on sale. It was being offered for a very cheap price. I was very excited with the deal and wanted to buy the bungalow immediately, but Bhavana persuaded me to search for another one. She had a feeling that there was something wrong with that bungalow. I could not reason out her feeling, as I saw no visible reason to justify it, but she remained adamant. I felt dissatisfied with her reasoning. But after a few days we heard that the bungalow was going to get demolished, as the Government intended to take the land away for road widening. That was not known to us, and was not even disclosed by the agent. Today I realize why Bhavana receives her messages the way she does. But how do I know what type I belong to?"

"You are for sure not Dr. Feelings, as you were not able to relate to Bhavana," said the genie, winking at Karmant.

"Yes, yes… I get your sarcasm! I think I am Ms. Eyes. That is because I tend to believe things more quickly when I see them. I love to read books, and I understand them better than if I listen to the same text on audio recording. Yes! I am most receptive to the things that I see."

"That's great. Once you know your medium, you can be more aware of it and strengthen it further. In this way you can help God to help you better."

"Help God to help me better? What do you mean, Genie?"

"I'll tell you seven steps for helping God to help you. Listen carefully. Since you are Ms. Eyes, I'll show you visuals to help you to learn the lessons more quickly. Here we go."

The genie drew a picture of a shop and a customer in the air.

"What is this picture about?" asked the genie, looking at Karmant.

"It's a shop, and the customer has come to purchase some stuff."

"Right. This is the first step, where God is a shopkeeper and you are a customer. He is the giver and you are a receiver. Ask Him for the things you need and take all that He gives you in life. Don't compare what He gives you with what He gives to others. Don't bargain with Him. God wants only love and faith from you. Whether they are difficulties or problems, or anything that troubles you, accept everything from Him with love and faith."

The genie flipped away the picture of the shop as if it were a puffy cloud and drew a picture of a smiling old man.

"What is this?"

"He is an old man who has a beautiful smile. He looks poor, though."

"Yes. Although he is old and poor, he has a warm smile on his face. What do you feel when you look at him?"

"He looks content with whatever he has."

"Right. In the second step, whatever you do, do it with a smile. In these days people have forgotten to smile or even laugh. Make sure that everything you do is with a warm smile of appreciation. When you do so, you convey to Him that you are happy with whatever He has given you. You assure Him that whatever He is doing is the right thing for you. You accept Him without any conditions."

"It's true; I had forgotten to smile. I only yelled and got angry. I wonder what it must have been to see a face like mine every day."

"Yes. But you need a deeper understanding of what a true smile is. A smile is a divine expression which has become corrupt today. You must step ahead of the smile which is limited to the lips only. The real smile arises from the heart, when a person knows who he actually is. Have a smile that reflects your discriminative intelligence. When your intelligence is used for the right cause, your level of awareness elevates. Learn to laugh at your own mistakes, as this will take you closer to your heart. Don't laugh at others, but laugh with others. Let the awareness of your laughter increase."

24

The genie waved away the second picture in a puff of smoke and drew a big lock and key.

"This is a lock and key. Looks like you want me to unlock something."

"You are right! In the third step, unlock all the channels through which God sends His guidance to you. Develop and maintain good relationships with the people around you, as they are the channels through which God sends His message. People often judge themselves by their intentions and others by their actions. It should be just the opposite. Look at your actions when you deal with yourself and look at others' intentions when you deal with them. When you learn to do this, you can connect to others' hearts, and your relationships will open up and blossom. When you have good relationships with people around you, everything sent by God reaches you easily. But when your relationships are strained, you close the doors, and information doesn't reach you."

"Ha… I know just what you mean. At one time I desperately wanted a book. I searched for it online and in bookstores, but had no luck. The book was available only in the United States. I happened to visit my neighbor's house for some reason and was surprised to see that book lying on his table. He told me that his nephew got that book on his last business trip to the United States and forgot it at his place last night. As his nephew was going to collect it after a few days, I was able to borrow the book from him. As I had good relations with my neighbor, I could get the book."

"Very well understood, Karmant. So, let's look at the fourth step now."

The genie drew a picture of someone sitting under a tree.

"Can you guess who this is?"

Karmant paused for a while and said, "I am not sure of who he is."

"Very well. I will give you a clue." The genie drew apples on the tree, with an apple falling from the air to the ground.

"Ah… the Law of Gravitation! Isaac Newton."

"Right. Your fourth step is to decode a message from this name."

"Newton… new ton… new… turn? Yes! NEW TURN. Is that right?" asked Karmant with a brilliant smile of achievement.

"Ah, look at your smile. That reflects intelligence indeed. You are right. In step four, learn to decode the messages that are constantly passed onto us by God and create something new. If you remain stuck in old beliefs and patterns, you fail to decode these divine messages and live a constricted, mechanical life. If you become flexible and are open to new ideas, you experience new things, and that brings a new turn into your life. 'New-turn' does not necessarily mean new creation. It can mean looking at the same thing differently, from a different perspective."

The genie looked up towards the sky with a smile. At that very moment Karmant's mobile phone started to ring.

"Who could be calling me at this time?" asked Karmant with a concerned look, fidgeting to remove the mobile phone from his back pocket. "Nobody would call me at this time… I think it's a wrong number…! Hello? Who is this?"

"You have just found out the fifth step!" said the genie from the other end of the phone.

Karmant pressed the End Call button on his phone and, looking up sheepishly at the genie, asked, "Is the fifth step 'wrong number'?"

"No, Karmant. In the fifth step, listen to your wise inner voice in order to receive divine guidance. Listen to your intuition: it is tuition from within you. Learn to listen to your intuition, just like you did now. You had the intuition that it would be a wrong number and it indeed was. As you develop this skill, you can help God to help you receive things more rapidly. You can experiment with this by listening to yourself. For example, before you answer your mobile phone or the doorbell or even before you read a letter, ask yourself who it could be. Look for the answers from the wise voice within you. Start seeking guidance for smaller issues first. As you become expert at this with regular practice, confidently seek guidance for major decisions. Recognize the action signals given by nature."

"That sounds marvelous, Genie. I can start practicing this from tomorrow," Karmant exclaimed with child-like eagerness.

Now the genie drew a white blank page on the backdrop of the dark sparkling sky.

"Blank paper!?" exclaimed Karmant.

"Yes, your next step is to be a blank page. And your exercise is not to fill in the blanks, but to feel in the blank."

"How can you feel in the blank? What exercise is this?"

"Learn to receive the signature of God on blank paper. Understand that God signs only on blank paper. Become a blank page by giving up your ego and purifying your mind from all negativities. Stop the unnecessary talk that you have with yourself. This only crowds your blank paper with words, which is meaningless, and leaves no place for God to leave any message for you. You may wonder how this can be achieved. The answer is by not being selfish in nature; don't always think of 'I'. Learn to set your mind right when it talks rubbish. Never derive any negative meaning out of any situation or any talk. In this way, you will be able to keep your paper completely clean and make space for God's signature."

Karmant nodded in agreement. Smiling at Karmant, the genie drew the last picture in the sky. It was a huge stony pyramid covering the entire sky.

"That's a pyramid," exclaimed Karmant, trying to decode the message.

"Yes. The final step is to build a pyramid. The pyramid represents prayer and meditation. Use these two elements together to build an internal pyramid that will connect you with God. It points above to the pinnacle of supreme life; to the supreme method of communicating with God and helping Him to help you in return.

Just as you want to spend time with your family, God too wants to be alone with you for some time everyday. It's like you have an appointment with God. During prayer, you communicate with God, and when you meditate after prayer God converses with you.

I was sent to you because God heard your prayers. So pray to Him every day. Prayer is the best form of communication, and a powerful tool. It can neither be misunderstood, nor can it go wrong at any time because of a shortfall of any technique. When you pray, God listens to you and gives you all that you want, although it could be through a different course.

You must keep faith in your prayers. Otherwise, the human mind falters when it sees that prayers are not fulfilled in the way that it wants, and negative thoughts hinder the fructification of prayers.

You prayed for these lessons and you got them; although you got them through a medium you would not have chosen. It was through demotion that you understood the seriousness of all these lessons. So always trust your communication with God. He knows what is best for you and how to give it to you. Believe in your prayers and communicate with God.

Prayer and meditation connect you with God and elevate your level of awareness. When every prayer is offered with love and gratitude, and every message of God is imbibed with loving and grateful receptivity, then your level of consciousness starts elevating towards the highest point. With these practices, you not only solve your personal problems but help resolve the problems of the entire planet. Understand that no problem can be resolved at the same level of awareness from which it originated. Be in communion with God with the help of these seven steps of communication. These steps will help God to hold your hand and lead you to the supreme levels of understanding and of knowing who you are and what role you should play in your life."

Karmant tried to control his tears. "Genie, you have changed my life today. I always thought I had some connection with the stars above, with God, with my family and my life. I always knew that life had some meaning and purpose to it. But I was not able to decode this message until you gave it to me today. Due to my lack of receptivity and lowered self-awareness, I didn't receive any positive message that came my way. Thank you, friend."

"Okay, Karmant. Now, it's time for me to leave. Let's meet tomorrow." The genie quickly disappeared.

Lost in contemplation on what he had gathered that day, Karmant didn't realize when he reached home.

25

When Karmant woke up in the morning he remembered the genie's lesson on impersonal goals, and wrote his new impersonal goal in his diary.

An innovator in the field of human excellence who helps others release their potential exponentially, so that the level of happiness and productivity in the world multiplies.

He read it aloud and experienced an inner surge of joy and fulfillment. He had never experienced such a positive energy during all his years in the industry. He heard a voice within say: this feeling of energy you have is what working for God is all about. He wondered: Is this the way God communicates with me?! This means I am a combination of Mr. Ears and Ms. Eyes. I need to be sensitive towards words and sights to decode signals sent by God. He set his mind to practice the seven steps of communication with God for the rest of the day.

He noted the seven steps in his diary.

Step 1 – Form a relationship with God. He is the giver and you are a receiver. Ask Him for the things you need and accept everything from Him with love and faith, without bargaining with Him or comparing what you have with what He gives to others.

Step 2 – Whatever you do, do it with a smile. By doing so, you convey to Him that you are happy with whatever He has given to you.

Step 3 – Unlock all the channels through which God sends His message to you.

Step 4 – Become like Newton and learn to decode the messages that are constantly passed onto you by God to create something new.

Step 5 – Awaken the wise inner voice. Listen to your intuition.

Step 6 – Learn to receive the signature of God on blank paper. You can become blank paper by giving up your ego and purifying yourself from negativity.

Step 7 – Build an internal pyramid of prayer and meditation to connect with God.

He prayed from the bottom of his heart, "O God, let me be in tune with you. Let my body become an instrument to fulfill your will. Please help me to accomplish the impersonal goal I have set for myself."

Jubilant and smiling, he entered the kitchen. Bhavana was busy preparing breakfast.

"Good morning, Bhavana!"

The warmth that Karmant exuded touched her, and she felt exhilarated. "Good morning, dear!"

"How is the preparation for the trip going?"

It was an unexpected question for Bhavana. Hesitantly she replied, "I have made a list of items to be bought. Could you accompany me to a shopping mall to buy them?"

"Yes, I will come with you," Karmant promised. Bhavana couldn't believe her ears. Busy Karmant never paid attention to such petty household issues in the past. She was overjoyed by his words. Karmant could sense her joy and felt happy.

When Karmant and Bhavana were about to leave for shopping, his phone rang. Mr. Desai was on the line.

"Hello Karmant. Sorry to disturb you during your holiday."

"No problem, Mr. Desai. What's the matter? Is there anything urgent to be addressed?"

"Yes, Karmant. Kevin called early this morning to say that he is hard-pressed by his management to deliver within ten days instead of the agreed fifteen days. We need to assess the feasibility. Will it be possible for you to join us in the board room at 11:30?"

"Yes, Sir. I will be there in an hour," Karmant reluctantly replied.

A feeling of frustration started mounting in him. He thought: "Why me? All my colleagues took off a while ago to be with their family, but I prioritized work over family and spent all my time working. I have been ruthless with my family all this time. Now that I have the chance to correct myself, why God is playing with me this way?"

Suddenly the thought of God reminded him of the first step of communication with God: to accept God's will with love and faith. He accepted the situation and felt relief from the burden on his head. Now he was able to look at the same situation from a different perspective. He decided to negotiate for a short break of two days instead of a weeklong vacation with Mr. Desai. By doing this, he would be able to strike a balance between his family and work. His mood again turned positive.

Now, the toughest job was in store for him: convincing Bhavana. Bhavana had seen his face become frustrated during his talk with Mr. Desai, but soon saw his expression mellow. She thought to herself, "He is no longer the old Karmant. Something has definitely transpired in him to change so drastically. God, thank you so much for bringing about this change in him."

Karmant composed himself. "Bhavana, please don't misunderstand me. I truly wanted to spend some quality time with you and Raju. That's why I had planned for this weeklong vacation. Something has suddenly come up in the office which needs my immediate attention, but I am trying to negotiate for a short break of two days. Are you okay with it?"

Bhavana was happy to see Karmant's deep concern for her feelings. She consoled him, "Karmant, don't worry. Take it easy. I am in no hurry. The vacation can wait. Attend to your work."

Karmant could feel Bhavana's unconditional love and care. "I have been able to focus on my job only because of Bhavana's unconditional support in taking care of the home. She has always been with me, through the ups and downs of my life. Indeed, God is helping me through her. I feel sorry that I have been taking her for granted. Gone is the past, from here on I will take care of my family." He remembered step 3: Unlock all the channels through which God sends His message to you. Filled with a deep sense of gratitude, he said, "Bhavana, thank you for being so considerate. I will try to strike a balance between work and home." Karmant could see a change in her body language. He realized that she was a mix of Dr. Feelings and Mr. Ears.

As Karmant left for the office he remembered: Whatever you do, do it with a smile. "Oh, that's the fifth step: to listen to the wise inner voice. That voice is reminding me of the second step." Karmant was so amazed by the way God was communicating with him, he barely realized when he had reached the office. He wondered, "How beautiful life can be when I am connected with God!" A prayer arose within him: "O God, please make me your blank paper. Let your signature alone shine on it." He closed his eyes and meditated for some time. When he closed his eyes, he sensed a gush of joy, love and peace within him. He realized that it was the seventh step, the pyramid.

Jay and Mr. Desai were awestruck to see a euphoric Karmant enter the board room. They had thought that asking him to cancel his holiday would make for an uncomfortable situation.

"Hello, everyone!" Karmant greeted them joyously.

"Hi Karmant! It's good to see you," Mr. Desai greeted him in return, trying to find words to communicate with him. "Karmant, if you don't mind, could you go on holiday after ten days? Mr. Kevin is really hard-pressed for an earlier delivery."

Karmant replied with confidence and composure, "Mr. Desai, I weighed my personal goal of taking my family on vacation against the goal of completing the deliverables for Kevin. I know how hard it was to regain the business with Kevin. I have always given priority to work over my family so far, but now I want to strike a balance between the two, without short-changing anyone. I have promised my little Raju a vacation, so I will take a short break of two days before I resume work. I hope you agree with this?"

Mr. Desai was pleased with his frank and honest communication. "Okay, Karmant. Go ahead and enjoy the short break. Meanwhile I will coordinate with Jay to get some basic things done from the team so that you can take it forward once you return."

Karmant was overjoyed. "Thank you, Mr. Desai. Thank you so much. During my break I might get some time to contemplate what I want to do with my future, and how I can bring my higher vision into action. My renewed focus will surely help the organization."

Mr. Desai and Jay were flabbergasted at Karmant's response. "Karmant, you were so rigid earlier. You couldn't convey things at the right time, in the right way. You were weak at human relations. But now you have become so flexible, and you excel in your communication. You have learned to be patient and caring. What made you change so drastically? Can you share the secret with others? We need such positive-minded people in our organization. In fact, we have an upcoming opening for the head of the HR department…"

Karmant decoded the signal. He thought to himself, "This looks like a very good beginning towards my higher vision."

He remembered he needed to give a passive response. "Mr. Desai, thanks for your kind words. It's my pleasure to share my experience with others. I will surely think over your suggestion and let you know. I need to take leave now. Goodbye." Jay and Mr. Desai looked at each other in disbelief as he left the room.

Karmant immediately contacted the travel helpdesk to cancel his planned vacation. Instead, he booked for two days at a nearby hill resort. He was happy that he could negotiate for time with his family without compromising on work commitments. He thought of informing Bhavana, but he kept it as a surprise for her.

On his way back home he was reflecting on the wondrous support he had received from everyone and counting the grace bestowed upon him. He thanked the genie from the bottom of his heart. Without the priceless wisdom received from the genie such miracles wouldn't have been possible in his life. He remembered his impersonal goal, and just by remembering it he sensed a stream of energy within him. It was as if his inner voice was prompting him to go ahead and help others release their potential exponentially so that the level of happiness and productivity in the world would multiply. The newfound purpose in his life was driving him.

Epilogue

On reaching home Karmant informed Bhavana about the two-day break he had been able to arrange. She was ecstatic. He felt happy just looking at her exuberance. For the rest of the day he was busy shopping with her and making arrangements for their travel.

At night, after ensuring that Bhavana and Raju were fast asleep, he slowly tiptoed towards the beach. He was eager to update the genie on how he had worked on communication with God. He meditated for some time, the familiar laughter rang in the air. The genie arrived with a loud guffaw.

"So, Karmant, are you ready for our final lesson today?"

"Final lesson!? What do you mean?" The sound came from Karmant's inner core.

The genie silently nodded.

Karmant was perplexed at this unexpected end to their conversations. With mixed feelings of pleasure and sorrow he replied, "Genie, without your wisdom, my life would have been miserable. I would have been a failure at home as well as in the workplace. You taught me to look at life in a new way. The incidents which used to plague and deceive me no longer make me unhappy. I can be happy amidst all circumstances. I want to spread this knowledge to everyone."

The genie was pleased with his words. "Then what's the problem?"

Karmant continued, "If you are giving me the last lesson today, then how can I get further guidance from you?"

The genie laughed loudly. "Not from me, but from the Source."

Karmant was baffled. "How can I seek guidance from the Source? I am thoroughly confused now. Could you please explain?"

"When you are on your heart, you connect to the Source and seek guidance from God. He opens your eyes to unseen and even miraculous opportunities and insights. Let God open your heart. Let the Source work through you."

"Do you mean to say that by practicing the seven steps of communication with God, I was connecting with the Source and allowing it to work through me?"

"Yes, Karmant. In fact, from day one I have been guiding you to do that. I believe that man is capable of creating miracles for himself. I just helped you achieve all your goals and overcome your difficulties with the help of right changes in your thoughts and attitude. I taught you the principles of natural communication and effortless productivity. You took all those lessons seriously and sincerely practiced them in your day-to-day life. As a result, the Source is working through you."

"Yes, Genie. Thank you so much for your guidance. I am planning to write blogs, articles, and books to document this knowledge, so that people all over the world can benefit from it. With this knowledge, they too will overcome the hurdles in their life and unleash their hidden potential exponentially. By connecting with the Source and allowing it to work through them, their work will become worship for God. As more and more people do this, the level of happiness, love, peace and productivity in the world will multiply. That is how I will fulfill my impersonal goal."

"Karmant, I am happy to hear that you have reflected on the action plan for your impersonal goal. Let's summarize the points covered in our discussions so far so as to make your task easier."

"Yes, Genie."

"We saw four ways of solving any problem. Do you remember them?"

"Yes! I remember them very well. The four ways are:

a. Whenever we face something which does not interest us, we quit it.

b. We change something in the current situation.

c. In any unpleasant situation we should use the mantra, 'Can I accept it?' When we accept a situation it no longer troubles us.

d. We should change our perspective towards the problematic situation. When we look at the same situation from a higher perspective, we will realize that it is helping us develop intellectually, to learn things required for our future, and to become prepared physically as well as mentally."

"That's great, Karmant! You really do remember it very well. We discussed positive self-talk, myths about success, and what true success is. Do you want to add anything to it?"

"Yes. True success is to feel complete and content from within. When you achieve this, irrespective of the status of your activities, you will progress towards your highest potential."

"Good. We also discussed how to meditate by numbering your thoughts."

"Yes, I've practiced this meditation every day in order to meet up with you."

"We discussed what anger is, and how to take charge of it."

"Anger is punishing ourselves for others' mistakes."

"Well said, Karmant. Anger is not always destructive. You can use anger constructively. Some of the techniques for getting rid of anger are: take a deep breath; give people a chance to explain their mistakes or their opinion before you speak; try to step into others' shoes to see their reasoning; and practice forgiveness."

"Yes, I've started practicing forgiveness since then. Every night I seek forgiveness from all the people whom I hurt and forgive those who hurt me."

"Keep up this practice, Karmant. We discussed five different types of responses. Can you name them?"

"Genie, they are: quick and impulsive response, rash or aggressive response, patient and analytical response, placative or passive response, and complete or awakened response."

"Good. We discussed conflict management and the best ways to effectively communicate during conflict."

"Yes, Genie. We discussed some ways—diffuse anger, place ourselves in the other person's shoes, take responsibility for our feelings, and respect the other person—to effectively communicate during conflict."

"We discussed verbal and non-verbal communication, their myths, choice of right words during verbal communication, and congruency in words, thoughts, actions, and feelings."

"Yes, Genie. You also gave me tips on parenting. That really helped me to improve my communication with Raju."

"Good. We talked about how to work unconditionally and impersonally and how to have a supreme and divine communication with God."

"Yes. There are three different ways of receiving guidance from God: Mr. Ears, Ms. Eyes, and Dr. Feelings. We also discussed seven steps of communication with God."

"Yes, and the last one we discussed was about allowing the Source to work through you."

"Yes, Genie. Thank you for the recap."

"Okay, it's time for me to go now and help someone else. I wish you all the best! Be always in communion with the Source."

"I am filled with gratitude for you, Genie. I am short of words to express how grateful I am. Thank you so much for all the help. You have given me more than enough but still if I want to get in touch with you, what should I do?"

The genie flashed his enigmatic smile, "Just utter my name a few times and see what happens. Try it now…"

"Your name is something like Jeoid, right?"

"Karmant, you forgot my name. My name is Jeeodee."

"Sorry, I do remember that you had mentioned your name but I had forgotten it. So, here we go. Jeeodee… Jeeodee… Jee o dee… Jee o dee…"

"What alphabets are you ending up pronouncing?"

"Jee..o..dee… G..o..d. Oh my God, it's 'GOD'. God, God, God"

Karmant felt centered at heart. He experienced the same gush of love, joy and peace that he experienced after meditation.

"So, are you God?"

"Karmant, my name reminds one of 'God'. 'God' is another name for the Source. I am just an external manifestation of the inner experience of the Source. During all these days, you have practiced the thought-numbering meditation to connect with me. Henceforth, practice it to access the Source within you and the Source will guide you. You can also chant G-O-D, G-O-D if it helps in meditating. Any meditation that helps the mind drop will help you connect to the Source."

Karmant's heart was filled with gratitude. "Thank you God for showering so much grace on me. Thank you for guiding me and taking me ashore. Thank you for always being with me. Let this body be instrumental to experience the Source and express its divine qualities."

With a loud guffaw the genie vanished into the unknown realm from where he had arrived.

"Thank you Genie. Thank you G O D. Good-bye…"

Karmant felt ecstatic, looking forward to a new beginning. He looked at the stars above and whispered, "Thank you for bringing the twinkle back into my life." He continued gazing into the empty sky. Watching the stars filled him with bliss. He took out his diary and penned down some words for his twinkling friends—

When I watch you twinkle your way
I see you giving light in every little way.
At all times, in all eternity
I learnt to shine like you today
while I face any extremity
in the midst of each day.

৩ ৩ ৩

:You can mail your opinion or feedback on this book to books.feedback@tejgyan.org

About Sirshree

Sirshree's spiritual quest, which began during his childhood, led him on a journey through various schools of philosophy and meditation practices. He studied a wide range of literature on mind science and spirituality. After a long period of deep contemplation on the truth of life, his quest culminated in attaining the ultimate truth.

Sirshree espouses, "All spiritual paths that lead to the truth begin differently but culminate at the same point – Understanding. This understanding is complete in itself. Listening to this understanding is enough to attain the Truth." Over the last two decades, he has dedicated his life to raise mass consciousness.

Sirshree has delivered more than 4000 discourses that throw light on this understanding. He has designed a system for wisdom, which makes it accessible to all. This system has inspired people from all walks of life to progress on their journey of the Truth. Thousands of seekers join in a virtual prayer for World Peace and Global Healing daily at 9:09 am and 9:09 pm.

About Tej Gyan Foundation

Tej Gyan Foundation is a non-profit organization founded on the teachings of Sirshree. The Foundation disseminates Tejgyan – the wisdom that guides one from self-development to Self-realization, leading towards Self-stabilization.

The Foundation's system for imparting wisdom has been assessed by international quality auditors and accredited with the ISO 9001:2015 certification. This wisdom has been presented in a simple, systematic, and practically applicable form that makes it accessible to people from all walks of life, regardless of religion, caste, social strata, country, or belief system.

The Foundation has centers in more than 400 cities and towns across India and other countries. The mission of Tej Gyan Foundation is to create a highly evolved society by leading seekers from negative thoughts to positive thoughts and further, from positive thoughts to Happy thoughts. A 'Happy thought' is the auspicious thought of being free from all thoughts, leading to the state of supreme bliss beyond thoughts.

If you seek such wisdom that leads you beyond mere knowledge, dissolves all problems, frees you from all limiting beliefs, reveals the true nature of divinity, and establishes you in the ultimate truth, then it is time to discover Tejgyan; it is time to rise above the mundane knowledge of words and experience Tejgyan!

The MahaAasmani Magic of Awakening Retreat

Self-development to Self-realization towards Self-stabilization

Do you wish to experience unconditional happiness that is not dependent on any reason? Happiness that is permanent and only increases with time? Do you wish to experience love, peace, self-belief, harmony in relationships, prosperity, and true contentment? Do you wish to progress in all facets of your life, viz. physical, mental, social, financial, and spiritual?

If you seek answers to these questions and are thirsty for the ultimate truth, then you are welcome to participate in the MahaAasmani Magic of Awakening retreat organized by Tej Gyan Foundation. This is the Foundation's flagship retreat based on the teachings of Sirshree.

The purpose of this retreat

The purpose of this retreat is that every human being should:

- Discover the answer to "Who am I" and "Why am I?" through direct experience and be established in ultimate bliss.

- Learn the art of living in the present, free from the burden of the past and the anxiety of the future.

- Acquire practical tools to help quieten the chattering mind and dissolve problems.

- Discover missing links in the practices of Meditation (*Dhyana*), Action (*Karma*), Wisdom (*Gyana*), and Devotion (*Bhakti*).

About Books by Sirshree

Sirshree's published work includes more than 150 book titles, some of which have been translated into more than 10 languages. His literature provides a profound reading on various topics of practical living and unravels the missing links in karma, wisdom, devotion, meditation, and consciousness.

His books have been published by leading publishing houses like Penguin, Hay House, Bloomsbury, Wisdom Tree, Jaico, etc. "The Source" book series, authored by Sirshree, has sold over 10 million copies. Various luminaries and celebrities like His Holiness the Dalai Lama, publishers Mr. Reid Tracy, Ms. Tami Simon and Yoga Master Dr. B. K. S. Iyengar have released Sirshree's books and lauded his work.

The Source
Attain Both, Inner Peace and Worldly success

Awaken the Power of Faith
Discover the 7 Principles of the Highest Power of the Universe

To order books authored by Sirshree, login to:
www.gethappythoughts.org
For further details, call: +91 9011013210

Tej Gyan Foundation – Contact details

Registered Office:
Happy Thoughts Building, Vikrant Complex, Near Tapovan Mandir, Pimpri, Pune 411017, INDIA. Contact: +91 20-27411240, +91 20-27412576

MaNaN Ashram:
Survey No. 43, Sanas Nagar, Nandoshi Gaon, Kirkatwadi Phata, Off Sinhagad Road, Taluka Haveli, Pune district - 411024, INDIA. Contact: +91 992100 8060.

WORLD PEACE PRAYER

Divine Light of Love, Bliss, and Peace is Showering;

The Golden Light of Higher Consciousness is Rising;

All negativity on Earth is Dissolving;

Everyone is in Peace and Blissfully Shining;

O God, Gratitude for Everything!

Members of Tej Gyan Foundation have been offering this impersonal mass prayer for many years. Those who are happy can offer this prayer. Those feeling low or suffering from illness can receive healing with this prayer.

If you are feeling troubled or sick, please sit to receive the healing effect of this prayer. Visualize that the divine white healing light is being showered on earth through the prayers of thousands and is also reaching you, bringing you peace and good health. You can dwell in this feeling for some time and then offer your gratitude to those offering the prayer.

A Humble Appeal

More than a million peace lovers pray for World Peace and Global Healing every morning and evening at 9:09. Also, a prayer (in Hindi) to elevate consciousness is webcast every day on YouTube at 3:30 pm and 9:00 pm IST. Please participate in this noble endeavor.

www.ingramcontent.com/pod-product-compliance
Lightning Source LLC
LaVergne TN
LVHW040150080526
838202LV00042B/3093